Introduction to UNIX and Linux Lab Manual

Introduction to UNIX and Linux Lab Manual

Catherine Creary
Lee M. Cottrell

McGraw-Hill/Osborne

New York Chicago San Francisco Lisbon London Madrid
Mexico City Milan New Delhi San Juan Seoul Singapore
Sydney Toronto

McGraw-Hill/Osborne
2600 Tenth Street
Berkeley, California 94710
U.S.A.

To arrange bulk purchase discounts for sales promotions, premiums, or fund-raisers, please contact **McGraw-Hill**/Osborne at the above address. For information on translations or book distributors outside the U.S.A., please see the International Contact Information page immediately following the index of this book.

Introduction to UNIX and Linux Lab Manual

4567890 FGR FGR 019876

ISBN 0-07-222694-3

Publisher
Brandon A. Nordin

Vice President & Associate Publisher
Scott Rogers

Acquisitions Editor
Chris Johnson

Executive Project Editor
Janet Walden

Acquisitions Coordinator
Athena Honore

Technical Editor
Walter Merchant

Project Manager
Laurie Stewart,
Happenstance Type-O-Rama

Copy Editor
Lunaea Weatherstone

Compositor
Jeffrey Wilson,
Happenstance Type-O-Rama

Proofreader
Sachi Guzman

Indexer
Jack Lewis

Series Designer
Maureen Forys,
Happenstance Type-O-Rama

Cover Series Design
Greg Scott

This book was composed with QuarkXPress™.

To Dean—thank you for your endless patience and support.

—Catherine Creary

This book is for Christopher, our "little big man." The short time you have been in my life has been a blessing.

—Lee M. Cottrell

Contents

About the Authors

Catherine Creary is an independent technical trainer, entrepreneur, and author. She currently holds a Bachelor of Education, MCT, MCSE, MCSA, and MCDBA. Catherine has more than 12 years of experience in the field of education. She is the author of *Network+ All-in-One Lab Manual* (McGraw-Hill/Osborne, 2002), *MCSE Windows XP Professional Lab Manual, Student Edition* (McGraw-Hill/Osborne, 2002), numerous training courses (Digital Think), an Exchange 2000 columnist (*www.OutlookExchange.com*), and several articles regarding cross-border employment for IT personnel. She has extensive experience in computer training, including development of adult education computer courses and curriculum design.

Lee M. Cottrell has been teaching networking, hardware, and computer programming at the Bradford School in Pittsburgh for eight years. In addition to teaching, Lee advises students, maintains the school's networks and computer equipment, and writes curricula for ten Bradford Schools. He is the author of *Windows 2000 Directory Services Administration Lab Manual*, *MCSE Windows 2000 Server Lab Manual*, and several Instructor's Manuals.

Lee graduated magna cum laude from the University of Pittsburgh with a Bachelor of Science in Pure Mathematics. Afterward, he enrolled in the Pitt Graduate School of Education and received a Professional Certificate and certification to teach mathematics in Pennsylvania high schools. Most recently, he completed a Master of Science in Information Science from the University of Pittsburgh. Lee can be reached at *lee_cottrell@hotmail.com.*

Acknowledgments

Thanks first and foremost to Chris Johnson, Athena Honore, and all the others at McGraw-Hill/Osborne who worked hard at putting this book together. Also, thanks to Walt Merchant for his invaluable technical edits.

Thanks to my agent Neil Salkind at Studio B Productions Ltd. (*www.studiob.com*), Jessica Richards, and all the staff at Studio B. Thanks to Jon Hirsch, Letham Burns, and Mitch Tulloch (*www.mtit.com*), three of the nicest computer geeks I know.

—Catherine Creary

I would like to thank the following people for all their help in preparing this book:

- Chris Johnson, Athena Honore, and all of the hard-working people at Osborne Media Group for encouraging me to be a better writer.

- Lunaea Weatherstone and Laurie Stewart for converting my prose into readable English.

- Walt Merchant for his excellent advice and finding my mistakes.

- The students, staff, and faculty at Bradford School for putting up with my moods during this project.

—Lee M. Cottrell

Introduction

Welcome to the *Introduction to UNIX and Linux Lab Manual* that accompanies your *Introduction to UNIX and Linux* (xiv, 2002). This lab manual is organized into chapters that map to the chapters of the study guide. There may be several lab exercises per chapter.

Each chapter includes a chapter introduction, a materials list, and setup instructions for each lab, as well as the lab exercises. The labs themselves include hands-on activities, and administration and troubleshooting questions. The labs will prepare you for possible real-life scenarios that you may encounter with UNIX/Linux.

Each chapter also has five Lab Analysis questions and a Key Term Quiz that allow you to demonstrate your knowledge of the material covered in the chapter. Finally, the chapter concludes with a brief summary of the key points. Step-by-step solutions to the lab exercises are found at the end of each chapter.

IN THIS LAB MANUAL

This lab manual provides the necessary exposure and training you'll need to master using UNIX or Linux. Topics that are covered include:

- Using UNIX/Linux utilities
- Creating files with the Visual Editor
- Getting help in UNIX/Linux
- Writing shell scripts
- Managing files and directories
- Setting file permissions
- Using the X Window System
- Using the multitasking features of UNIX/Linux
- Administering UNIX/Linux users

After the completion of this lab manual, you will have a better understanding of the UNIX/Linux infrastructure and be capable of managing its daily operations.

Lab Exercises

Understanding the theory behind networking and UNIX/Linux principles is important for a network administrator. The question is, can you transfer this knowledge to a system situation?

Each lab exercise allows you to apply and practice a particular concept or skill in a real-world scenario.

CASE STUDIES

Each objective is presented as a case study. They provide a conceptual opportunity to apply your newly developed knowledge.

LEARNING OBJECTIVES

Working hand in hand with the study guide, one objective is to help you understand UNIX/Linux. The second objective is to have you develop critical thinking. In networking, not all installations, reinstallations, or network and system problems present themselves in the same way each time. To this end, you need to be able to analyze, consider your options and the result of each option, and select and implement that option. If it works, great; if it doesn't, you start over again.

LAB MATERIALS AND SETUP

To fully accomplish each lab, it is necessary that the hardware and software requirements below be met. If this is not possible, then read through the steps and become familiar with the procedures as best you can.

The screen shots and directions in this book correspond to Red Hat Linux 7.3. All of the exercises can be performed on a workstation installation of Red Hat. Most likely, other versions of UNIX/Linux will work with the steps presented. Typically, only minor changes are evident between versions.

Your computer must be compatible with Red Hat or another version of Linux. Most likely, your computer is compatible. For Red Hat verification, see *www.redhat.com* for the complete Hardware Compatibility List. The following lists the minimum supported specifications for Red Hat Linux 7.3. More RAM and a faster processor will result in a better Linux system.

32MB of RAM

80386 processor or higher

VGA monitor or better

Mouse or other pointing device

4x or faster CD ROM

One or more hard drives with a minimum of 4GB free space

Network card (optional)

Dial-up or LAN connection to the Internet

GETTING DOWN TO BUSINESS

The hands-on portion of each lab is step by step, not click by click. Steps provide explanations and instructions, walking you through each task.

Lab Analysis Test

These are questions to quickly assess your comprehension of what you've learned in the study guide and each lab in the chapter. The answers should be in your own words. This shows that you've synthesized the information and you have a comprehensive understanding of the key concepts.

Key Term Quiz

These are technical words that you should be able to recognize, and you should know their definitions and purpose. This will help you on the job.

Solutions

Each chapter provides solutions for the Lab Exercises. These solutions are meant to compare your lab procedures with the correct lab procedures. If you are familiar with UNIX/Linux, you will find that in certain parts of the lab exercises there is more than one way to accomplish the step. The end result—and understanding the process to reach that end result—is the main objective.

Chapter 1

Logging On to the System

Lab Exercises

UNIX/Linux computers can serve many users at the same time. Each user must have an account that uniquely identifies them on the system. An administrator must create a unique account for each user so they can be granted secure access to the system. Then the user can enter their unique login name that is associated with their account, and the password that matches that login account. If the information is correctly entered into the system, the user will be granted access. If an error is made upon entering the login name or password, the user will be refused access to the computer.

This chapter examines the process of logging on to a Linux system. You will successfully log on to a system and view the terminal window and graphical window environments that Linux provides. You will test the login process by entering login information incorrectly and observe how Linux responds to login errors. You will also research the Internet for careers that require knowledge of UNIX/Linux systems, versions of UNIX/Linux that are available, and use of each system in today's society and business world.

 20 MINUTES

Lab Exercise 1.01: Logging On to a Linux System

Matthew has recently installed Red Hat Linux 7.3 on his laptop computer. He has never used the Linux operating system before, but is very familiar with several Windows operating systems. He needs to familiarize himself with the login process and both the graphical and terminal windows that are available to him once he logs on to the system.

Learning Objectives

In this lab, you will be logging on to a Red Hat Linux 7.3 computer. By the end of this lab, you'll be able to:

- Log on to a Linux system
- Examine the graphical window environment
- Start and activate a terminal window
- Log off a Linux system
- Test incorrect login errors

Lab Materials and Setup

The materials you need for this lab are:

- Computer with Red Hat Linux 7.3 installed with a graphical window environment
- Pencil and paper
- Password for the *root* login account

Getting Down to Business

These steps guide you in logging on to a Linux system, testing login errors, and viewing the graphical environment. You will also have to apply the knowledge that you acquired in the *Introduction to UNIX and Linux* textbook by John Muster (McGraw-Hill/Osborne, 2002) for starting and activating a terminal window.

Step 1   From your Linux computer, enter the *root* login account at the login banner prompt. Were you prompted for a password?

_____

_____

✖ **Warning**

It is unwise to use the administrative *root* login account except for specific tasks, and then only very carefully. However, for the purposes of this lab you will simply be learning the log on and log off process and you will not be administering the system in any way.

Step 2 Enter the associated password for the *root* account that you established during the installation of the operating system. Did the password appear on the screen? Were you able to successfully log on to the system?

_____

_____

✔ **Hint**

You should receive a warning message on the screen regarding using the *root* login account.

Step 3 At the desktop of your Linux computer, observe the icons, menus, and programs that are available. Start and activate a terminal window. What text appears in the terminal window?

_____

_____

Step 4 Exit the terminal window. Log off the Linux computer.

Step 5 Log on to the Linux computer in the graphical environment with the login name of *Matthew* and the password of wrkwrk. Were you successful in logging on to the system? Why or why not? Note any error message that appears.

_____

_____

 60 MINUTES

Lab Exercise 1.02: Exploring UNIX and Linux

Ann is using a Linux computer for the first time. She comes from a Windows background and is unsure of how learning Linux will help in her job search. She is unaware of the uses for UNIX/Linux and the versions of each system that are currently in use in her city and around the world. She has asked for your help in researching the Internet to acquire knowledge on these topics.

Learning Objectives

In this exercise, you explore the uses of UNIX/Linux systems through browsing the Internet. After you complete this lab, you will be able to:

- Identify career opportunities requiring UNIX/Linux
- Identify uses for UNIX/Linux systems
- Identify different versions of UNIX
- Differentiate between UNIX, Linux, and DOS commands

Lab Materials and Setup

For this lab exercise, you'll need:

- Computer with Red Hat Linux 7.3 installed
- Access to the Internet with a web browser
- Pencil and paper

Getting Down to Business

The following steps guide you in exploring the uses of UNIX and Linux in today's society.

Step 1   Log on to the Linux computer using the **root** account and password.

Step 2   Open a web browser and search the Internet for careers that require knowledge of the UNIX or Linux operating systems. List your results in the space provided.

_____

_____

Step 3   Research the Internet for common uses of the UNIX and Linux systems around the world. Include government infrastructures, academic institutions, and corporate networks.

Step 4   Research the Internet to obtain the names of different versions of UNIX that you may encounter in the information technology industry.

Lab Analysis Test

1. What common mistakes are made when entering either the login name or password that may result in an incorrect login? List five common mistakes.

   _____

   _____

2. What functions do UNIX/Linux servers provide in today's business world?

   _____

   _____

3. What steps enable you to start and activate a terminal window from the graphical desktop environment?

   _____

   _____

4. What are the advantages and disadvantages of using the **root** login account?

   _____

   _____

5. What is the result of entering a correct login name versus entering an incorrect login name at a login prompt?

   _____

   _____

Key Term Quiz

Use the following vocabulary terms to complete the sentences below. Not all of the terms will be used.

    exit

    graphical window

    login banner

    login name

    password

    root

    Teletype device

    terminal

1.   The login named _____ is the account used to administer the system that has authority over system events and operations.

2.   Entry into a UNIX/Linux system is granted only when a user provides both a _____ and the associated password that match an established user on the system.

3.   After starting a UNIX/Linux computer, you are typically greeted with a _____, either in the terminal or graphical window.

4.   Typing your login name or password in uppercase letters results in a computer treating your terminal as a _____.

5.   The _____ command is a UNIX/Linux message that results in the closure of a terminal window.

Lab Wrap-Up

One of the main features of a Linux computer is that several users can be logged on to the system at the same time. Now that you have completed this lab, you should have successfully logged on to a Linux computer and you should be familiar with the various desktop environments that are configurable with Linux. You should also have tested the security of a Linux system by committing errors when entering a login name and password. Linux security should have prevented access to the system as a result of these errors.

Solutions

In this section, you'll find solutions to the Lab Exercises.

Lab Solution 1.01

Helping Matthew to familiarize himself with the login process, as well as the graphical and terminal windows, should have involved these steps:

Step 1   After entering the **root** login account at the login prompt, a second prompt will appear, asking you to enter the associated password for the login account.

Step 2   The associated password for the **root** login account will vary according to each system. This password should have been established during the installation of your Linux operating system. This password will not appear on the screen as you type in a terminal window; however, a series of asterisks will appear in the graphical window, representing the password that you type. After successfully entering the correct associated password, Linux will log the user onto the system and the desktop environment will be displayed.

Step 3   You should have started a terminal window by selecting and clicking on the monitor icon that is present on the panel. The terminal window should have appeared and you should have activated the terminal by clicking your mouse anywhere in the terminal window. You should be greeted by a prompt in the terminal window that contains your login account.

Step 4   You should have exited the terminal window by typing **exit** at the prompt. The terminal window should have closed, leaving you viewing the graphical window environment. You should have chosen the *log off* selection from the menu and successfully logged off the system.

Step 5   Because the Matthew account and associated password do not exist in the system, you should have been denied access. You should have received an `Authentication Failed` message and the login field should reappear.

Lab Solution 1.02

The following steps should guide you in exploring the UNIX and Linux operating systems:

Step 1   You should have successfully logged on to the Linux computer using the **root** account and password.

Step 2   You should have opened a web browser and found that some of the careers that require knowledge of the UNIX or Linux operating systems include UNIX/Linux administrators, programmers, developers, scripters, analysts, engineers, trainers, instructors, and so on.

Step 3   You should have researched the Internet for common uses of the UNIX and Linux systems around the world and found that government infrastructures use UNIX/Linux for several different purposes. You can read an article regarding the use of Linux in the U.S. government at *http://www.linuxworld.com/linuxworld/lw-2001-01/lw-01-government.html*. Academic institutions use UNIX/Linux severs for hosting academic records and creating large area networks. Corporate networks use UNIX/Linux for web servers, application servers, and so on. Financial institutions and markets also use UNIX to host their critical data.

Step 4   You should have researched the Internet to obtain the names of different versions of UNIX. These include Digital UNIX, Hewlett-Packard HP-UX, IBM AIX, SCO UnixWare, SGI IRIX, and Sun Solaris. Flavors of UNIX can be found at *http://www.unix-systems.org/ what_is_unix/flavors_of_unix.html*.

Chapter 2

Touring the System

Lab Exercises

Working on a UNIX/Linux computer usually involves creating and saving files that are important to your business. In order to successfully organize these files, you must understand how the system responds to commands. This chapter examines the process of interacting with the shell in Linux by executing utility commands and arguments to change directories and filenames, remove and copy files, and display file contents.

By the end of this chapter, you will have successfully explored and managed the file system through working with several utilities and interacting directly with the shell.

In the second part of this lab chapter, you will sharpen your help skills. LaTrina has asked you to help her learn more UNIX. She understands that you have a life outside of her web site. She asks you to teach her how to use the help system on UNIX so she can attempt to answer her own questions. You reply that the help system is composed of several pieces. **man** pages provide the technical details of a command, with little verbiage. The **info** utility accesses a large document providing details and clear explanations of a command. Both are useful in obtaining help in UNIX.

 30 MINUTES

Lab Exercise 2.01: Working with the Shell

Joel is unsure whether his assistant has created the monthly calendar for his restaurant, the Temple of Meat. This calendar is used to create a work schedule for all employees of the restaurant. If he cannot locate the file in his current directory, he wants to create a file that consists of a calendar for the month of November 2002.

Learning Objectives

In this lab, you will issue commands and arguments within the shell of a Linux computer. By the end of this lab, you'll be able to:

- Create a user account

- List files in the current directory

- Issue a command with an argument

- Direct the output of a utility to a file

- Verify file creation and content

Lab Materials and Setup

The materials you need for this lab are:

- Computer with Red Hat Linux 7.3 installed

- Pencil and paper

Getting Down to Business

The following steps guide you in creating a new user account for the purpose of this and future labs. You will also have to apply the knowledge that you acquired in the *Introduction to UNIX and Linux* textbook by John Muster (McGraw-Hill/Osborne, 2002) for working with the shell.

✔ **Hint**

UNIX systems usually have an online manual that can be consulted to list options and to learn more about utilities. At any time you can consult the manual by executing the **man** command followed by the name of a utility.

Your computer might boot to text mode. If this is the case, execute the command **startx** to enter Gnome.

Step 1   Log on to the Linux computer using the *root* login account and password.

Step 2   From the *Programs | System* menu, select the *User Manager* program. The Red Hat *User Manager* console opens.

Step 3   Click the *New User* button and create a new user account for yourself with the attributes provided here:

> **Username** First Name
>
> **Full Name** First Name Last Name
>
> **Password** 16110FF

Step 4   Figure 2-1 shows several user accounts. Click *OK* and close the *User Manager* console. Log off the computer.

Step 5   Log on to the computer using the new user account and password that you created for yourself.

Step 6   Open a terminal window and verify that the prompt indicates your user login account. At the prompt, list the files that are in your current home directory. Are there any files listed?

_____

_____

Step 7   At the prompt, issue a command and argument that creates a file called *november_work_schedule* that contains the calendar for the month of November 2002. Note the command in the space provided.

_____

_____

Step 8   Verify that the *november_work_schedule* file was created by viewing the list of files in the current directory. Did the newly created file appear listed?

_____

_____

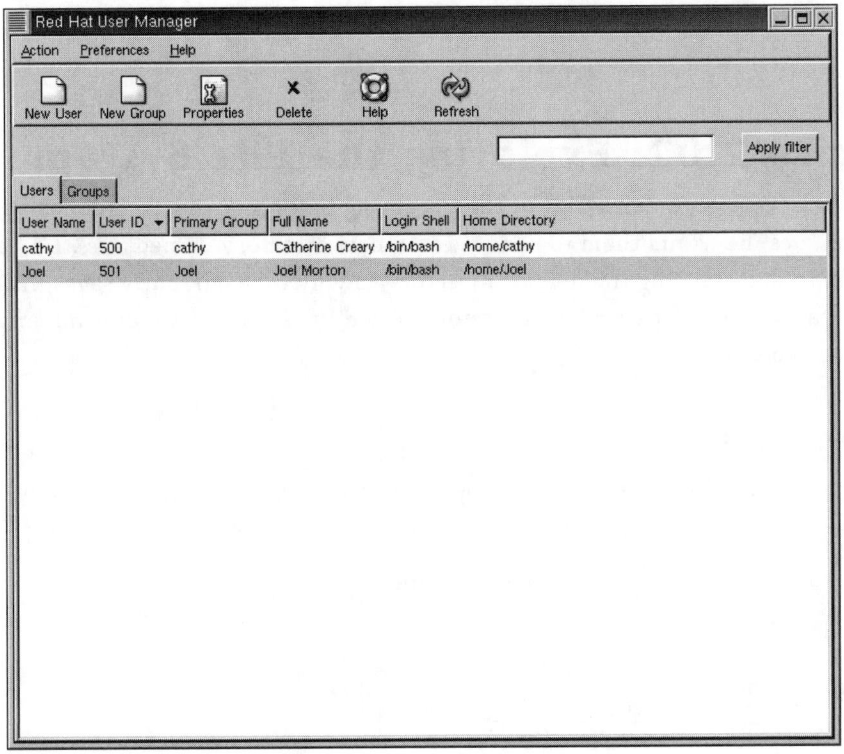

Figure 2-1 Sample user accounts created with *User Manager*

Step 9 Verify that the contents of the *november_work_schedule* file consists of the calendar for the month of November 2002. Are the contents of the file correct? Log off the computer.

 30 MINUTES

Lab Exercise 2.02: Exploring the File System

Dean needs to create several new sales files in the upcoming three months. In order to better organize these new files, he wants them to be saved in a new directory named *Sales*. He has asked for your help in determining the default directory in which he currently saves his files. He wants to learn how to create a new directory, as well as how to save, append, and access files in this directory.

Learning Objectives

In this exercise, you will explore the file system by examining the directory structure in Linux. After you've completed this lab, you will be able to:

- Identify your current location in the file system

- Create a new directory

- Change directories

- Create and append a file in a subdirectory

Lab Materials and Setup

The materials you need for this lab are:

- Computer with Red Hat Linux 7.3 installed

- Pencil and paper

Getting Down to Business

The following steps guide you in creating and saving a file in a new subdirectory. You will also have to apply the knowledge that you acquired in the *Introduction to UNIX and Linux* textbook by John Muster (McGraw-Hill/Osborne, 2002) for working with the shell.

Step 1   Log on to the Linux computer with your username and password. Open a terminal window.

Step 2 At the prompt, type the command that provides you with your current location in the file system. Record the name of the directory in the space provided.

_____

_____

✔ **Hint**

The current location is also known as your working directory.

Step 3 At the prompt, type the command that creates a subdirectory of your current directory named _Sales_. Confirm that the subdirectory has been created.

Step 4 Type the command that changes your current location in the file system to the _Sales_ subdirectory. Confirm that you are now located in the new _Sales_ subdirectory.

Step 5 Create a new file named _Sales.date_ in the _Sales_ subdirectory by directing the output of the **date** utility to the file. Verify that the _Sales.date_ file exists in the subdirectory. Append the _Sales.date_ file with the 2002 calendar.

Step 6 Change your current location back to your home directory. Verify that the change occurred. Log off the computer.

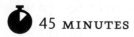 45 MINUTES

Lab Exercise 2.03: Using Utilities to Manage Files

Keogh Insurance has just hired Lisa as an administrative assistant. Her first assigned task is to create and save several files in her home directory for future use. She has asked you to teach her how to use the Linux utilities to copy, print, and generally manage these files. You have chosen to demonstrate the utilities on various sample files that you will create.

Learning Objectives

In this lab, you will create several files and manage them with the Linux utilities. After you complete this lab, you will be able to:

- Create and append files in your home directory

- Copy files to a subdirectory

- Remove a file with confirmation

- Rename, print, and move a file

Lab Materials and Setup

For this lab exercise, you'll need:

- Computer with Red Hat Linux 7.3 installed

- Pencil and paper

- *Sales* subdirectory (created in Lab 2.02)

Getting Down to Business

The following steps guide you in creating several files. You will also have to apply the knowledge that you acquired in the *Introduction to UNIX and Linux* textbook by John Muster (McGraw-Hill/Osborne, 2002) for using utilities to manage files.

Step 1 Log on to the Linux computer with your username and password. Open a terminal window.

Step 2 Create the following files in your home directory:

Filename	File Content
Car_insurance	All current online users

Filename	File Content
Travel_insurance	Current date
House_insurance	September 2001 calendar
Life_insurance	List of all files in the current directory
Health_insurance	List of all processes associated with your login account

---

✔ **Hint**

You will have to type the correct commands at the prompt that create the above files with the appropriate content.

Step 3   Verify that all files have been created. Display the contents of the *Travel_insurance* file. Append the contents of the file by adding the calendar for the current month and year to the file.

Step 4   Copy the *Car_insurance* file to the *Sales* subdirectory that you created in Lab 2.02. Rename the *House_insurance* file to *House*.

Step 5   Remove the *Health_insurance* file with a confirmation. What is the argument used to prompt for a confirmation?

_____

_____

Step 6   Attempt to print the *Life_insurance* file to a printer that you specify.

✖ **Warning**

Ensure that you do **not** have an available printer for this lab exercise.

Did you receive an error message? Log off the computer.

_____

_____

 10 MINUTES

Lab Exercise 2.04: Using man to Learn the Function of Switches

The first stop on the help tour is **man**, an online copy of the entire *UNIX Programmers Manual*. The **man** utility is good at providing quick, technical details about commands. It provides every technical tidbit for every UNIX command. You will access the **man** pages for several commands and write the function of their switches.

Learning Objectives

Upon completion of this lab, you will be able to use **man** to access technical information about a command.

Lab Materials and Setup

You will need the following to complete this lab:

- An account on a UNIX/Linux computer
- A pen or pencil

Getting Down to Business

Define the following switches using the **man** pages for the command. Using your own words, write the description the **man** page provides in the Description column.

Command	Switch	Description
bash	-r	_____
chmod	-v	_____
cp	-l	_____
grep	-c	_____
ls	-d	_____

Command	Switch	Description
man	-k	_____
mkdir	-m	_____
ps	-r	_____
sort	-r	_____
wc	-L	_____

 10 MINUTES

Lab Exercise 2.05: Using man to Find Pages by Keyword

LaTrina is not entirely impressed with **man**. The problem, she says, is that you need to know the command before you can get help. This only helps a UNIX guru, not a mere mortal. How can she search the **man** pages for keywords? For example, how can she find all commands that set permissions?

You know that **man** has a search option, **-k**, which allows you to search the **man** pages by string. This should impress LaTrina.

✖ Warning

On some versions of UNIX, the **catman -k** command sets the index in UNIX so that a user can search the **man** pages using key words.

Learning Objectives

Upon completion of this lab, you will be able to search the **man** pages for keywords.

Lab Materials and Setup

You will need the following to complete this lab:

- An account on a UNIX/Linux computer
- A pen or pencil

Getting Down to Business

You will use the **-k** switch for **man** to find the number of commands that deal with the following keywords. Please write the number of commands that pertain to each keyword in the Number of Commands column.

✔ Hint

You can use the **apropos** utility instead of **man -k**.

✔ **Hint**

Remember to redirect the output into **wc**. This will let UNIX count for you!

Keyword	Number of Commands
images	_____
modem	_____
permissions	_____
XII	_____

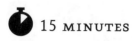 15 MINUTES

Lab Exercise 2.06: Using the info **Utility to Find Detailed Descriptions of Commands**

LaTrina is still not quite content. She is impressed with the ability to search the pages for keywords. However, she still thinks that **man** is not a good enough help system. She wants more information about a command: information that is written in plain English, not by UNIX geeks for other UNIX geeks. You decide to introduce her to the **info** utility.

Learning Objectives

Upon completion of this lab, you will be able to:

- Find the **info** database for a utility

- Browse the **info** database

Lab Materials and Setup

You will need the following to complete this lab:

- An account on a UNIX/Linux computer

- A pen or pencil

Getting Down to Business

> ✔ **Hint**
>
> You will run the **info** utility. This will open a menu-like interface. You will be able to move around the system using the arrow keys, SPACEBAR, PAGE DOWN, PAGE UP, and the ENTER key. The arrow and page keys perform as expected. The ENTER key opens the desired topic. SPACEBAR acts like the PAGE DOWN.

Run the **info** command and answer the following questions regarding each command. Write your answers in the space provided.

1.   What is the default sort order for **ls**?

   _____

   _____

2.   How does **chmod** handle symbolic links?

   _____

   _____

3.   What command do you need to run to create your own **info** file?

   _____

   _____

4.   Which invocation of **touch** writes any data in memory out to disk?

   _____

   _____

5.   The **dir** command is the equivalent of what set of **ls** switches?

   _____

   _____

 30 MINUTES

Lab Exercise 2.07: Finding Answers to UNIX/Linux Questions Online

LaTrina is convinced that the UNIX/Linux help is worthwhile. She has worked with it enough to stop pestering you for a while. Unfortunately, other friends have started asking you questions about UNIX/Linux. Many of the questions are very technical and require a specific answer. The only place to find these answers is the Web.

A competent computer user is always hammered with questions. The better you answer the questions, the more frequently the questions arrive. This is a double-edged sword. You gain the respect and admiration of your peers and colleagues, while losing the ability to be productive.

Learning Objectives

Upon completion of this lab, you will be able to find answers to UNIX/Linux questions using the Internet as a source of information and direction.

Lab Materials and Setup

You will need the following to complete this lab:

- An account on a UNIX/Linux PC that has access to the Internet

- A pen or pencil

Getting Down to Business

You know that a good place to start is the home page for the company that provided the software. Thus, if you are asked a question, you should start at **www.redhat.com**. Here is a list of common sites:

Linux Manufacturer	Web Site
FreeBSD	**www.freebsd.com**
Mandrake	**www.mandrake.com**

Linux Manufacturer	Web Site
Red Hat	*www.redhat.com*
Slack Ware	*www.slackware.com*
SuSE	*www.suse.com*
Sun Solaris	*www.sun.com* or *docs.sun.com*

If the manufacturer site is no help, try *www.google.com* or another search engine. Enter the key terms in the question into the search box, and check the results.

Find a web page that answers the following questions. Write the URL in the space provided.

1. How can I configure a printer in my Red Hat 7.3 Linux installation?

_____

_____

2. What modems are supported in my Mandrake 7.0 installation?

_____

_____

3. I need to contact FreeBSD about a security hole discovered in the software. Whom do I contact?

_____

_____

4. What is the current version of the KDE?

_____

_____

5. What is a good "newbie" site for UNIX?

_____

_____

Lab Analysis Test

Answer each of the following questions in a short sentence or paragraph. There may be more than one right answer.

1. What are two ways of using the **mv** utility to manage files and directories?

2. What two UNIX commands are available for sending a file to a printer? Why will only one command work on your system?

3. What utilities are available to display the contents of a file?

4. How are redirection pipes used when executing commands with utilities?

5. What system directories are displayed as a result of executing the **ls /** command?

6.   What is displayed if you request **info** on a utility with no **.info** file?

_____

_____

7.   What is the purpose of the **man** pages?

_____

_____

8.   What is the difference between the **help** utility and the **info** utility? (You may want to run **help**.)

_____

_____

9.   What is the option used by **man** to search keywords?

_____

_____

10.   What does the command **chown** do?

_____

_____

Key Term Quiz

Use the following vocabulary terms to complete the sentences below. Not all of the terms will be used.

apropos	argument
b	cat
d	cd
info	command
-k	lp
keyword	lpr
l	option
man	rm -i
n	shell
p	utility
u	

1. The _____ command deletes an indicated file, but asks the user to confirm the deletion.

2. The _____ is a program that enables you to give the system instructions, also known as commands.

3. When you type the command **date**, and press ENTER, you are instructing the shell to run the date _____.

4. A(n) _____ is an option or flag that provides specific instructions to a utility.

5. Simply entering the _____ command will change your current directory to the home directory.

6. The _____ command provides the manual pages for a command.

7. The _____ utility provides an in-depth description about a utility.

8. The _____ switch for **man** can search through the **man** pages for a utility.

9. When in **info**, you use the _____ key to display the previous node.

10. Apropos will search the **man** pages by _____.

Lab Wrap-Up

One of the main features of a Linux computer is that several users can be logged on to the system at the same time, but each user has a separate default directory in which to save their files so that no overlapping exists. By now, you should have successfully explored and worked with the file system to create and manage files. You should also be familiar with several utilities and the effect of using these utilities to print, copy, move, remove, and view your files and file structure.

Congratulations! You have learned how to use the help system in UNIX/Linux. The **man** command provides the technical description of every command in UNIX/Linux. It provides all switches, all parameters, and a little description of each. The **info** utility provides a better description for each command. It provides an English description of the command, as well as an interface that is easy to navigate in.

This knowledge will serve you well in the workplace. An employee who can learn on his or her own is a much-desired employee. Since you know how to use **man** and **info**, you will be less likely to need technical support or guidance. This makes you efficient and cost effective, which are both good traits for all employees.

In the next lab, you will learn how to use the multitasking features of UNIX/Linux. You will learn how to run multiple commands, determine what commands your friends are running, and how to stop those jobs that have stopped responding. Help will be of great use.

Solutions

In this section, you'll find solutions to the Lab Exercises.

Lab Solution 2.01

Helping Joel to familiarize himself with the shell and create a new file should have involved the following steps:

Step 1 You should have logged on to the Linux computer using the **root** administrative login account and password. This account gives you the authority to create additional user accounts.

Step 2 You should have opened the **User Manager** console by selecting it from the **System** menu on your Linux computer.

Step 3 You should have created a user account for yourself that included your first name as the username, your first and last name as the full name, with a password of 1611oFF.

Step 4 In order to save the user account you created for yourself, you should have clicked the **OK** button and then closed the **User Manager** console and logged off the computer. This will prepare you to test the user account that you created by logging back on to the computer using the new username and password.

Step 5 You should have successfully logged on to the computer using the new user account and password that you created for yourself. If you were unsuccessful at logging on, make sure that you typed the information correctly at each prompt. If still unsuccessful, you can log back on to the computer using the administrative **root** account, and recreate or edit the user account to correct any errors.

Step 6 The terminal window prompt should indicate your user login account. This will help you recognize that when you search for files, you are searching in the correct home directory. After issuing the **ls** command, you should have found that there were no files present in your current directory.

Step 7 The correct command to issue at the prompt that would create a file called *november_work_schedule* containing the calendar for the month of November 2002 would be:

> **cal 11 2002 >** *november_work_schedule*

The **calendar** utility is used to create a result for the eleventh month (November) of 2002. This result is then directed to a file titled *november_work_schedule*.

Step 8 You should have issued the **ls** command to ensure that the *november_work_schedule* file was created. The filename should appear listed at the prompt.

Step 9   In order to verify that the content of the *november_work_schedule* file consists of the calendar for the month of November 2002, you should have issued the **more** *november_work_schedule* command. The calendar for the month of November should appear correctly at the prompt. The **more** command displays the contents of the file.

You should have successfully completed the lab and logged off the computer to prepare for the next lab exercise.

Lab Solution 2.02

The following steps should help Dean in exploring the file structure of his Linux computer:

Step 1   You should have successfully logged on to the Linux computer with your username and password and opened a terminal window from the panel.

Step 2   You should have typed the **pwd** command, which provides you with your current location (present working directory) in the file system.

Step 3   You should have typed the **mkdir** *Sales* command, to create a subdirectory named *Sales*. It will be a subdirectory of your personal home directory.

Step 4   You should have typed the **cd** *Sales* command to change from your current location in the file system to the *Sales* subdirectory. You should have successfully changed to the new subdirectory.

Step 5   You should have created a new file named *Sales.date* in the *Sales* subdirectory by directing the output of the **date** utility to the file with the following command:

> **date** > *Sales.date*

You should have appended the *Sales.date* file with the **cal 2002 >>** *Sales.date* command. As in Figure 2-2, issuing the **dir** command will verify that the *Sales.date* file has been created in the subdirectory.

Step 6   You should have typed either the **cd** or **cd /** command to change from your current location in the *Sales* subdirectory back to your home directory. The **cd** command will always take you directly to your home directory, whereas the **cd /** command will take you to the root directory of the file structure in which you are currently located. You should have verified that the change occurred by typing the **pwd** command.

You should have successfully completed the lab and logged off the computer in order to prepare for the next lab exercise.

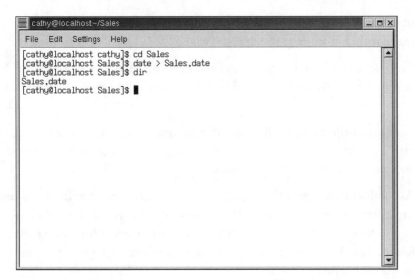

FIGURE 2-2 The *Sales.date* file appears in the *Sales* subdirectory

Lab Solution 2.03

The following steps indicate the correct use of utilities to manage files on your Linux computer:

Step 1 You should have successfully logged on to the Linux computer with your username and password and opened a terminal window.

Step 2 You should have created the following files in your home directory by typing the associated commands at the terminal prompt:

Filename	Command
Car_insurance	**who** > *Car_insurance*
Travel_insurance	**date** > *Travel_insurance*
House_insurance	**cal 9 2001** > *House_insurance*
Life_insurance	**ls** > *Life_insurance*
Health_insurance	**ps** > *Health_insurance*

Step 3 You should have verified that issuing the **ls** command created all files. To display the contents of the *Travel_insurance* file, you should have used the **more** *Travel_insurance* command.

Appending the contents of the file is accomplished by typing **cal xx xxxx >>** *Travel_insurance*, where **xx** is the current month and **xxxx** is the current year.

Step 4 To copy the *Car_insurance* file to the *Sales* subdirectory, you should have typed **cp** *Car_insurance Sales*. You rename the *House_insurance* file to *House* with the **mv** *House_insurance House* command.

Step 5 You should have typed the **rm -i** *Health_insurance* command to remove the *Health_insurance* file with a confirmation. The **-i** argument is the instruction to ask for confirmation before any filenames listed as other arguments.

Step 6 There are two possible commands that you could type to attempt to print a file to a printer. The **lp** and **lpr** utilities manage printers. The commands are system dependent so some systems may respond to one of the commands with an error message indicating that the command is not found. You should have received an error message if no printer was available. Figure 2-3 displays this error.

You should have successfully completed the lab and logged off the computer in order to prepare for the next lab exercise.

```
cathy@localhost:~/Sales                                           _ □ x

 File   Edit   Settings   Help
[cathy@localhost cathy]$ cd Sales
[cathy@localhost Sales]$ dir
Healthinsurance
[cathy@localhost Sales]$ lp Healthinsurance
Status Information:
 sending job 'cathy@localhost+465' to missingprinter@localhost
 connecting to 'localhost', attempt 1
 cannot open connection to localhost - No such file or directory
Make sure the remote host supports the LPD protocol
and accepts connections from this host and from non-privileged (>1023) ports
[cathy@localhost Sales]$ ▮
```

FIGURE 2-3 Printer error message is displayed

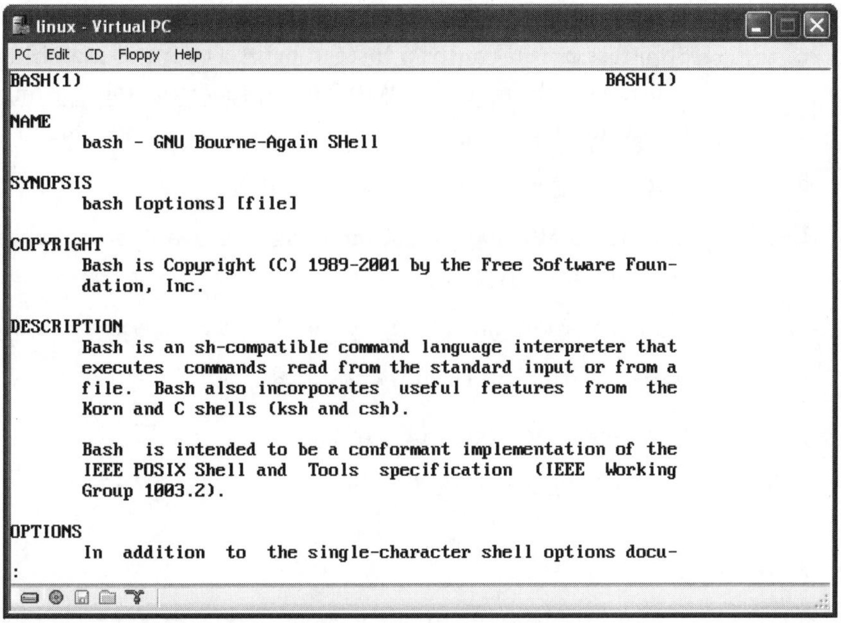

FIGURE 2-4 Typical **man** output

Lab Solution 2.04

To answer this lab, you will need to run the command **man**. For the first example, **man bash** will bring up the **man** page for **bash**. Press the SPACEBAR until you see the **-r** option. You can also search for the switches using the / key. Figure 2-4 shows a typical **man** output.

✔ **Hint**

The descriptions are copied from the Red Hat Linux 7.3 **man** pages.

Command	Switch	Description
bash	**-r**	If the **-r** option is present, the shell becomes restricted (see RESTRICTED SHELL).
chmod	**-v**	Output a diagnostic for every file processed.
cp	**-l**	Link files instead of copying.

Command	Switch	Description
grep	-c	Suppress normal output; instead print a count of matching lines for each input file. With the **-v**, invert-match option, count non-matching lines.
ls	-d	List directory entries instead of contents.
man	-k	Specify an alternate set of **man** pages to search based on the system name given.
mkdir	-m	Set permission mode (as in **chmod**), not **rwxrwxrwx -umask**.
ps	-r	Restrict output to running processes.
sort	-r	Reverse the result of comparisons.
wc	-L	Print the length of the longest line.

Lab Solution 2.05

To solve this lab, you will need to run the **man** utility and the **-k** switch. To simplify counting, you can redirect the output into **wc -l**. This will count the number of lines. Thus, for the images keyword, **man -k** *images* **| wc -l** would be the command entered.

Keyword	Number of Commands
images	46
modem	12
permissions	15
X11	18

Lab Solution 2.06

To solve each of the questions, you must use the **info** command. You will need to read the pages to find the answer. The text is based on Red Hat Linux 7.3, but should be similar on other versions of Linux. Figure 2-5 shows a typical output for **info**.

1.   Run the command **info ls**. The answer (ASCII) is under the **sort** option.

2.   Run the command **info chmod**. The answer (it does not ever change the permission of a symbolic link) can be found on the first page.

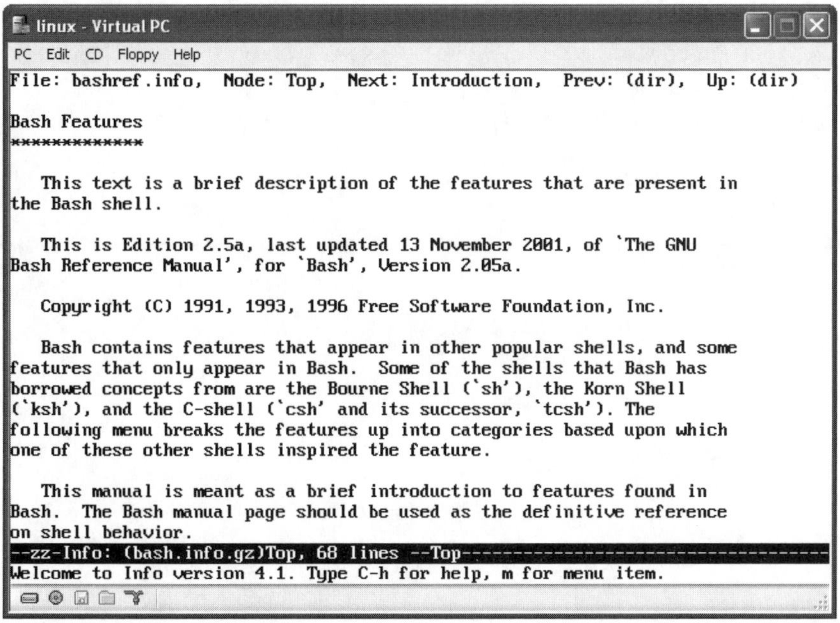

FIGURE 2-5 Typical **info** output

3. Run the command **info info**. The answer (makeinfo) can be found under the **Create an info file** option.

4. Run the command **info touch**. The answer (sync) can be found under the **sync invocation** option, which is the last page of the **info** database.

5. Run the command **info dir**. The answer should be visible on the first page. **dir** is equivalent to **ls -C -b**.

Lab Solution 2.07

The following pages will provide answers to the questions posed in Lab Exercise 2.07. By no means are these the only pages that will satisfy the requirements.

1. *www.redhat.com/docs/manuals/linux/RHL-7.3-Manual/custom-guide/ch-printing.html*

2. *www.linux-mandrake.com/en/en/fhard70.php3#modems*

3. *www.freebsd.org/security/index.html*

4. *www.kde.com*

5. *www.unixgeeks.org/security/newbie/unix/*

Chapter **3**

Touring Utilities, Shell Instructions, and Processes

Lab Exercises

In the previous chapters, you learned how UNIX/Linux computers use several utilities to locate system and user data and files. Once these files were located, you used utilities to manipulate the data. Manipulation of these files can be expanded by additional powerful utilities.

This chapter examines utilities that read input from files, changes the data that they read, and then sends the changed data to your screen, a file, or another utility. In the following labs, you instruct the shell where to connect input and output, employ special characters in command lines, and modify the user environment by customizing programs to meet your needs. You also change a password, and create and execute shell scripts to learn basic programming.

 30 MINUTES

Lab Exercise 3.01: Employing Powerful Utilities

Sam is writing a new novel and wants to organize the first three chapters he has written to ensure that they meet the specifications written in his contract. He wants to obtain a line, word, and character count of certain chapter files. He also needs to concatenate several chapter files to make sure the plot of the novel flows smoothly from chapter to chapter. To help him search through his chapters quickly, Sam would benefit from the ability to locate specific lines in a file, but he doesn't know how to do so. He has asked for your help in learning the capabilities of several Linux utilities.

Learning Objectives

In this lab, you organize a number of files on a Linux computer by employing powerful utilities. By the end of this lab, you'll be able to:

- Create a text file

- Count the elements of a file

- Sort and locate lines in a file

- Combine multiple files

Lab Materials and Setup

The materials you need for this lab are:

- Computer with Red Hat Linux 7.3 installed

- Pencil and paper

Getting Down to Business

The following steps guide you in employing powerful utilities to organize numerous files on a Linux computer. You will also have to apply the knowledge that you acquired in the *Introduction to UNIX and Linux* textbook by John Muster (McGraw-Hill/Osborne, 2002) for employing utilities to create and organize files.

Step 1   Log on to the Linux computer with your username and password. Open a terminal window.

Step 2   Use the **cat** utility to create Sam's chapter files in your home directory from the information provided here:

Chapter Title	Text
Chapter_1	It was a dark and stormy night.
	Christina unsuccessfully tried to block out the sounds of the thunderstorm.
Chapter_2	Christina looked at her watch.
	He was late.
Chapter_3	The sun was setting but Jake didn't care.

Step 3   Verify that all files were created in your home directory. For each chapter, verify the line, word, and character count. Note your results in the space provided.

Step 4   Create a file in your home directory named *ChapterList* that lists the names of the first three chapters in your home directory. Sort the file in reverse order and note the results in the space provided.

_____

_____

Step 5   Locate the word *thunderstorm* in the appropriate chapter by employing the correct utility at your terminal screen. Locate the word *storm*. Do the results differ? Give reasons for your answer in the space provided.

_____

_____

Step 6   To review how the chapters of Sam's novel flow together, create a file named *Novel* that is a concatenation of the three chapter files. Display the contents of the *Novel* file on your screen to ensure that it successfully contains the text of all three chapters. Log off the computer.

 20 MINUTES

Lab Exercise 3.02: Managing Input and Output from Utilities

Sam has added a fourth chapter to his novel. He is unsure of whether he misspelled any words in the added text. He wants to check the spelling in the entire fourth chapter. He also wants to sort through the list of titles he is considering for his novel as he inputs the titles from his keyboard.

Learning Objectives

In this exercise, you manage input and output from utilities. After you've completed this lab, you will be able to:

- Specify a file as input

- List misspelled words from a file

- Sort several lines of input

Lab Materials and Setup

The materials you need for this lab are:

- Computer with Red Hat Linux 7.3 installed

- Pencil and paper

Getting Down to Business

The following steps guide you in managing input and output from utilities. You will have to apply the knowledge that you acquired in the *Introduction to UNIX and Linux* textbook by John Muster (McGraw-Hill/Osborne, 2002) for employing these utilities.

Step 1 Log on to the Linux computer with your username and password. Open a terminal window.

Step 2 Create a file named *Chapter_4* that contains the following text:

He knew that Christina was wateing for him on the other side of the country, yet he didn't feel the need to rush to meet her.

✔ **Hint**

Be sure to include the spelling mistake in the text for the *Chapter_4* file.

Step 3   Check the *Chapter_4* file for any spelling errors. Did the system return any errors?

_____

_____

Step 4   Input and sort the list of potential titles for Sam's novel:

Bad Attitudes

Love in Disguise

Never Enough

No Surprises

All or Nothing

What was the result of the sort?

_____

_____

Step 5   How does the command **sort** < *Chapter_4* differ from the command **sort** *Chapter_4*? Log off the computer.

_____

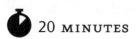 20 MINUTES

Lab Exercise 3.03: Working with Special Characters

Sam wants to search through his list of chapters easily, without having to type the complete name of every chapter he would like to search. He wants to employ special characters to save time. He also wants to ensure that he is mentioning characters' names often in each chapter so that readers will find it easy to follow the storyline. However, at certain times Sam needs the shell to not interpret special characters, but rather to treat them as ordinary characters. He is unsure how to accomplish his goals and has asked for your help.

Learning Objectives

In this exercise, you work with special characters. After you complete this lab, you will be able to:

- Use wildcards to replace characters

- Recognize shell and environment variables

- Prevent the shell from interpreting special characters

Lab Materials and Setup

For this lab exercise, you'll need:

- Computer with Red Hat Linux 7.3 installed

- Pencil and paper

- Successful completion of all previous labs

Getting Down to Business

The following steps guide you in working with special characters. You will have to apply the knowledge that you acquired in the *Introduction to UNIX and Linux* textbook by John Muster (McGraw-Hill/Osborne, 2002) for employing special characters in a command line.

Step 1 Log on to the Linux computer with your username and password. Open a terminal window.

Step 2   Enter the command **echo $HOME** at the prompt. What is the result of the command? What type of variable is used in the command?

_____

_____

Step 3   From your current directory, list all files within the directory that begin with the letter C. Note the command that you executed in the space provided.

_____

_____

Step 4   To help Sam search for character names in all chapters, execute a command that uses special characters and searches all files in the current directory. Note the correct command in the space provided below.

_____

_____

Step 5   To help prevent the shell from interpreting certain special characters, what instruction should Sam issue to the shell?

_____

_____

Step 6   Execute a command that instructs the shell to echo the sentence but not to interpret the wildcard characters in the following text:

Christina read the sign on the wall. It said ** BEWARE**.

Indicate the correct command in the space provided. Log off the computer.

_____

_____

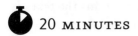 20 MINUTES

Lab Exercise 3.04: Modifying the User Environment

Sam has reached the point in his novel where he is happy with his *Novel* file and doesn't want to overwrite it by mistake. He wants to ensure that the output of a utility will not overwrite this file. Additionally, he wants help updating the password associated with his login account for security purposes.

Learning Objectives

In this exercise, you prevent overwriting a file and update a password. After you complete this lab, you will be able to:

- Instruct the shell not to overwrite a file

- Verify the status of a variable

- Change your login password

Lab Materials and Setup

For this lab exercise, you'll need:

- Computer with Red Hat Linux 7.3 installed

- Pencil and paper

- Successful completion of all previous labs

Getting Down to Business

The following steps guide you in modifying a user environment. You will also have to apply the knowledge that you acquired in the *Introduction to UNIX and Linux* textbook by John Muster (McGraw-Hill/Osborne, 2002) for preventing a utility from overwriting a file and changing a login password.

Step 1   Log on to the Linux computer with your username and password. Open a terminal window.

Step 2   Display the contents of the *Novel* file. Ensure that the *Novel* file contains the text of all four chapters of Sam's novel by updating the file to include each chapter file.

Step 3   Type the command that prevents utilities from overwriting files in your home directory. Verify that you have activated the variable and note both commands in the space provided.

_____

_____

Step 4   Attempt to update the contents of the *Novel* file by executing the command **date >** *Novel* to ensure that you are unable to make any changes to the file. Deactivate the variable to prepare for future labs.

Step 5   Enter the appropriate command that enables you to change your password and set your new password to MbfGW2002.

Step 6   Log off the computer. Attempt to log back on with your username and new password. Were you successful? Log off the computer.

 15 MINUTES

Lab Exercise 3.05: Creating Shell Scripts

Sam wants to create a script called *Workday* to keep track of the files in his directory. He wants to be able to execute this script daily as he adds new chapters to his novel. He also wants to keep track of the current date. He also requested that a calendar for the month of November be added to the script so he can reference it to ensure he meets his deadlines.

Learning Objectives

In this exercise, you create a shell script. After you complete this lab, you will be able to:

- Create a new script
- Add utilities to the script
- Change permissions on a file
- Save and execute a script

Lab Materials and Setup

For this lab exercise, you'll need:

- Computer with Red Hat Linux 7.3 installed
- Pencil and paper

Getting Down to Business

The following steps guide you in creating a shell script. You will have to apply the knowledge that you acquired in the *Introduction to UNIX and Linux* textbook by John Muster (McGraw-Hill/Osborne, 2002) for creating scripts.

Step 1   Log on to the Linux computer with your username and password. Open a terminal window.

✔ **Hint**

Remember that you should have changed your password to MbfGW2002 in the previous lab.

Step 2   At the prompt, type the following command to create a new file: **cat** > *Workday*.

Step 3   Create and save a script that includes the list of files in your home directory, the current date, and the monthly calendar for November 2002.

Step 4   Ensure that the permissions for the *Workday* file indicated that it is executable before attempting to run the script.

Step 5   Execute the script by typing the command *./Workday*. Note the results of the script in the space provided.

✔ **Hint**

If the command *./Workday* did not result in the script executing, make sure the permission on the *Workday* file is executable.

Lab Analysis Test

1. What is the result of attempting to change your password on a Red Hat Linux 7.3 computer to the word password?

    _____

    _____

2. Does the *noclobber* variable prevent files from being overwritten by users attempting to add text to files? Give reasons for your answer.

    _____

    _____

3. What are the seven fields that appear in the password file? Briefly list and define each field.

    _____

    _____

4. How would you create a file that concatenates the *Chapter_1*, *Chapter_2*, and *Chapter_3* files in reverse order?

    _____

    _____

5. What is the difference in output as a result of executing the CTRL-D and CTRL-C commands?

    _____

    _____

Key Term Quiz

Use the following vocabulary terms to complete the sentences below. Not all of the terms will be used.

awk

chmod

env

grep

$HOME

noclobber

sort

$USER

variable

wildcard

1. _____ is the variable that represents the location of your workspace directory.

2. A(n) _____ can represent a string of characters in a command.

3. The _____ command is used to change the permissions/mode of a file.

4. The variable named _____ can be used to prevent the output of a utility from overwriting a file.

5. The _____ variable displays an output that consists of some of the environment variables that are set for your shell.

Lab Wrap-Up

You should now be familiar with instructing the shell where to connect input and output, employing special characters in command lines, and modifying the user environment. You should also know how to change a password, and create and execute scripts.

Solutions

In this section, you'll find solutions to the Lab Exercises.

Lab Solution 3.01

The following steps should help Sam in organizing the chapter files of his novel:

Step 1   You should have successfully logged on to the Linux computer with your username and password and opened a terminal window.

Step 2   The **cat** utility can be used to create Sam's chapter files in your home directory. For *Chapter_1* you should have typed the following:

```
cat > Chapter_1
It was a dark and stormy night.
ENTER
Christina unsuccessfully tried to block out the sounds of the thunderstorm.
CTRL-D
```

To create *Chapter_2*, you should have typed the following:

```
cat > Chapter_2
Christina looked at her watch.
ENTER
He was late.
CTRL-D
```

To create *Chapter_3*, you should have typed the following:

```
cat > Chapter_3
The sun was setting but Jake didn't care.
CTRL-D
```

Step 3   You should have verified that all files were created in your home directory by typing the **ls** command. To retrieve the line, word, and character count for a chapter, the correct command would be **wc *filename***. This would produce the following results:

```
2    18    107        Chapter_1
2     8     44        Chapter_2
1     8     42        Chapter_3
```

Each line indicates the number of lines, words, and characters in the appropriate file.

Step 4   To create a combination file in your home directory named *ChapterList* that lists the names of the first three chapters, you should have used the **ls** utility. The correct command would be **ls > *ChapterList***. The results are displayed in Figure 3-1.

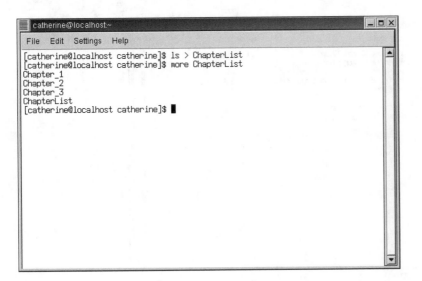

Figure 3-1 *ChapterList* file contents

This would create a file that joins the output of the list of all files in the directory into a single file. The order of the contents would coincide with the listed order of the filenames. To sort the file in reverse order you should execute the **sort** utility with the reverse argument: **sort -r** *ChapterList* **| more.**

Step 5   The **grep** utility can be used to locate a line in a file that contains a word or string of characters. To locate the word *thunderstorm* in the *Chapter_1* file:

```
grep thunderstorm Chapter_1
```

The results of the commands should list the text:

```
Christina unsuccessfully tried to block out the sounds of the thunderstorm.
```

To locate the word *storm* in the *Chapter_1* file:

```
grep storm Chapter_1
```

The results of the commands should list the text:

```
It was a dark and stormy night. Christina unsuccessfully tried to block out
the sounds of the thunderstorm.
```

The **grep** utility lists every line containing the string *storm*, therefore showing both the sentence containing the word *storm* and the sentence containing the word *thunderstorm*.

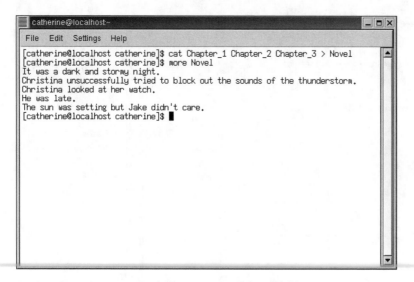

FIGURE 3-2 Concatenated chapters in the *Novel* file

Step 6   To create a file named *Novel* that is a concatenation of the three chapter files, you should have typed: **cat** *Chapter_1 Chapter_2 Chapter_3* **>** *Novel*. The **ls** command will display the contents of the *Novel* file on your screen as shown in Figure 3-2. You should have successfully logged off the computer.

Lab Solution 3.02

The following text should help Sam to manage input and output from utilities:

Step 1   You should have successfully logged on to the Linux computer with your username and password and opened a terminal window.

Step 2   To create the file named *Chapter_4*, you should have executed the command: **cat >** *Chapter_4* and then entered the text:

> He knew that Christina was wateing for him on the other side of the country,
> yet he didn't feel the need to rush to meet her.

Step 3   To check the *Chapter_4* file for spelling errors, you execute the command **spell <** *Chapter_4*. The system should have returned the word *wateing* spelled incorrectly. The **spell** command does not suggest a change for the word.

Step 4   To input and sort the list of potential titles for Sam's novel, you should have executed the command:

```
sort
Bad Attitudes
Love in Disguise
```

```
Never Enough
No Surprises
All or Nothing
CTRL-D
```

The sort order lists the potential titles in alphabetical order directly beneath the original list.

Step 5 The results from both commands (**sort** < *Chapter_4* and **sort** *Chapter_4*) are exactly the same as shown in Figure 3-3. You should have successfully completed this lab and logged off the computer.

Lab Solution 3.03

The following steps should guide Sam in working with special characters:

Step 1 You should have successfully logged on to the Linux computer with your username and password and opened a terminal window.

Step 2 By entering the command **echo $HOME** at the prompt, the result should display the current home directory of your login name. For example, the result may resemble:

```
/home/username
```

The *$HOME* variable is known as a shell variable. The shell obtained this variable when you logged on to the system.

```
catherine@localhost:~
File  Edit  Settings  Help
[catherine@localhost catherine]$ sort < Chapter_4
He knew that Christina was wateing for him on the other side of the country, yet
 he didn't feel the need to rush to meet her.
[catherine@localhost catherine]$ sort Chapter_4
He knew that Christina was wateing for him on the other side of the country, yet
 he didn't feel the need to rush to meet her.
[catherine@localhost catherine]$ ▮
```

Figure 3-3 Results of **sort** for two different commands

Step 3   At the command prompt, you should have executed the command **echo C***. The result is a listing of all filenames in the current directory that begin with the letter C.

Step 4   To help Sam search for character names in all chapters, you should have executed the command **grep** *Christina* * to find all results for the Christina character, and the **grep** *Jake* * command to find all results for the Jake character. The results should list the chapters that contain any reference to the characters.

Step 5   Sam should include a back slash (\ ) in front of any special character in order to help prevent the shell from interpreting the character. For example: **echo** *We can output a* * would present the result *We can output a* *.

Step 6   You should have executed the command:

```
echo Christina read the sign on the wall. It said \**BEWARE\**.
```

This command instructs the shell to echo the sentence but not to interpret the wildcard characters, resulting in the following output:

```
Christina read the sign on the wall. It said **BEWARE**.
```

You should have successfully completed the lab and logged off the computer.

Lab Solution 3.04

The following steps should guide you in preventing a file from being overwritten and updating your password:

Step 1   You should have successfully logged on to the Linux computer with your username and password and opened a terminal window.

Step 2   To display the contents of the *Novel* file, you should have executed the **more** *Novel* command. The current **Novel** file should only contain the text from the first three chapters of Sam's novel. You can update the *Novel* file to include the contents of *Chapter_4* by executing the **cat** *Novel Chapter_4* command. This command concatenates the two chapters.

Step 3   In order to prevent utilities from overwriting files in your home directory, you would execute the **set -o noclobber** command. To verify that you have activated the variable, you should have executed the **set -o** command. This will return a list of variables and their current status (**On/Off**). The *noclobber* variable should be set to **On**.

Step 4   You should have been unable to make any changes to the *Novel* file with the date utility as shown in Figure 3-4. You should have returned the *noclobber* variable to the setting of **Off** by executing the **set +o noclobber** command.

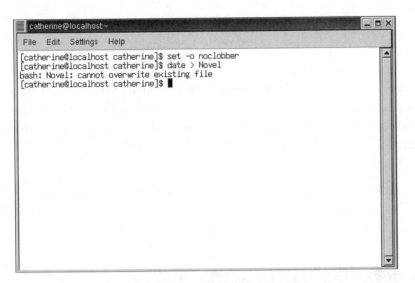

FIGURE 3-4 Results of turning the *noclobber* variable on

Step 5   To change your password, you should have simply executed the **passwd** command. You would have been prompted for your current password and you should have responded by typing in the password. You are then prompted for a new password. You should have then entered the new password of MbfGW2002. The program asks you to re-enter the new password. If done correctly you will not receive an error and the password will have been changed.

Step 6   You should have successfully logged on to the computer with your username and new password to confirm that you have indeed changed the password associated with your login account. After doing so, you will have successfully completed the lab and therefore can log off the system.

Lab Solution 3.05

The following steps should guide you in creating a shell script:

Step 1   You should have successfully logged on to the Linux computer with your username and password and opened a terminal window.

Step 2   At the prompt, typing the command **cat >** *Workday* creates a new file.

Step 3   A sample script that fulfills Sam's requirements would be:

```
echo My files to date are
ls
echo Today is
```

```
date
echo My deadlines are the 6th 13th and 24th
cal
CTRL-D
```

Step 4   To ensure that the permissions for the *Workday* file indicated that it is executable before attempting to run the script, you can view the file permission with the **ls -l** *Workday* command as shown in Figure 3-5. The file should not be executable, as it was just created, so you should have changed the permissions on the script to allow it to be executed by typing the **chmod +x** *Workday* command.

Step 5   After executing the script by typing the command *./Workday*, you should have received the output of the **ls**, **date**, and **cal** commands integrated with the text you have input. You should have successfully completed the lab and logged off the computer.

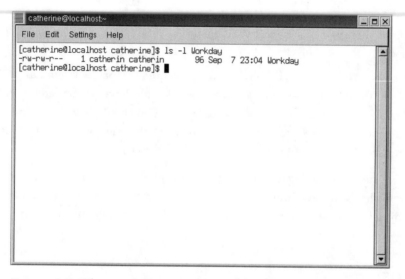

FIGURE 3-5 File permissions on the *Workday* file

Chapter 4

Editing with the Visual Editor

Lab Exercises

You should now be familiar with using utilities to create text files. You have worked with utilities that read input from files, change the data that they read, and then send the changed data to your screen, other files, or utilities. This chapter takes one step beyond using utilities to alter files and introduces the text editor known as the UNIX/Linux visual editor or **vi**.

The powerful **vi** editor allows a user to create text by giving all instructions through combinations of keystrokes. The visual editor allows users to access files, move through lines of text, edit content within files, and read in other files. The following labs are designed to familiarize you with the **vi** editor, its command mode and append mode, and all of the features and functions it provides.

 20 MINUTES

Lab Exercise 4.01: Working in an Existing File

Sam would like to explore the possibilities of using the visual editor for editing his novel. The *Novel* text file combines all chapters of the novel Sam has written to date. He would like to explore the command mode of the **vi** editor and navigate through the *Novel* file, searching for text to possibly delete due to the excessive length of the file.

Learning Objectives

In this lab, you explore the visual editor by working in an existing file. By the end of this lab, you'll be able to:

- Activate the visual editor tool
- Operate in command mode

- Move around in the text file

- Delete text and undo text changes

- Quit the visual editor tool

Lab Materials and Setup

The materials you need for this lab are:

- Computer with Red Hat Linux 7.3 installed

- Pencil and paper

- Successful completion of all previous labs

Getting Down to Business

The following steps guide you in exploring the visual editor features by working in an existing file. You will have to apply the knowledge that you acquired in the *Introduction to UNIX and Linux* textbook by John Muster (McGraw-Hill/Osborne, 2002) for editing with the visual editor.

Step 1   Log on to the Linux computer with your username and password. Open a terminal window.

✔ **Hint**

Remember that you should have changed your password to MbfGW2002 in a previous lab.

Step 2   Ensure that you have the *Novel* file in your home directory by listing the contents of the directory. Instruct the shell to open the *Novel* file so you can view the contents.

Step 3   Once you have viewed the contents of the file with the shell, open the *Novel* file with the visual editor. Do the contents of the file appear to be the same as when opened by the shell?

Step 4   Navigate through the *Novel* file by using the direction key that moves the cursor down one line at a time. Which two keys are available for moving down through the file one line at a time?

_____

_____

Step 5   Navigate in each direction through the file by using all of the direction keys available to you. List the keys and their associated directions in the space provided.

_____

_____

Step 6   Enter the command that instructs the visual editor to search through the *Novel* file, then locate and move the cursor to the word *the*. Once you have located the first occurrence of the word *the*, locate the next, and every other occurrence thereafter.

Step 7   Enter the command that instructs the visual editor to search through the *Novel* file, then locate and move the cursor to the word *rush*. Instruct the **vi** editor to delete the words *rush to* in the sentence.

Step 8   Navigate to the first line of text in the *Novel* file. Instruct the editor to delete the entire line of text. Instruct the **vi** editor to undo the previous change to the line of text.

Step 9   Save your edits to the *Novel* file and quit the visual editor. Confirm that you have exited the visual editor by issuing the **dir** command to the shell. Open the *Novel* file with the shell and view the contents of the file. Have your edits been saved? Log off the computer.

_____

_____

 30 MINUTES

Lab Exercise 4.02: Navigating Through a Text File

Sam has discovered that it takes him quite a long time to scroll through his *Novel* text file with the visual editor. Until now, he has been moving through the file by line and character. He would like to speed up the process of navigating through a file and has asked for your help in using augmented direction keys, line numbers, and targeted searches in order to do so.

Learning Objectives

In this exercise, you navigate through a text file with the visual editor. After you've completed this lab, you will be able to:

- Navigate through a text file by line and by character
- Explore augmented direction commands
- Work with line numbers
- Search a text file

Lab Materials and Setup

The materials you need for this lab are:

- Computer with Red Hat Linux 7.3 installed
- Pencil and paper

Getting Down to Business

The following steps guide you in exploring the visual editor features in append mode. You will have to apply the knowledge that you acquired in the *Introduction to UNIX and Linux* textbook by John Muster (McGraw-Hill/Osborne, 2002) for navigating through a text file with the visual editor.

Step 1 Log on to the Linux computer with your username and password. Open a terminal window.

Step 2 Open the *Novel* text file with the visual editor. Implement the use of augmented direction keys to navigate through the file according to the following instructions:

a) Move 4 lines down.

b) Move 6 spaces right.

c) Move 2 lines up.

d) Move 4 spaces left.

What is your final location in the text? Indicate the augmented direction keys or command used to arrive at each instructed location.

_____

_____

Step 3 Display the line numbers for each line of text in the *Novel* file. In the space provided, indicate the commands you would use to both display and turn off line numbers.

_____

_____

Step 4 Instruct the visual editor to go to the following specific lines of the *Novel* file:

a) Fourth line of the file

b) Last line of the file

c) Line 2

Indicate the commands you used for each of the above locations, and indicate any alternate commands that would provide the same result.

_____

_____

Step 5 Search through the *Novel* file according to the following instructions:

a) Move two lines down from current location.

b) Search for the letter *e*.

c)   Search backward through the file for the previous occurrence of the letter *e*.

d)   Move the cursor three words forward.

e)   Move the cursor to the end of the current line.

f)   Position the cursor at the highest line on the screen.

g)   Move the cursor to the last line of the file.

In the space provided, indicate the correct commands for each of the searches. Log off the computer.

_____

_____

 45 MINUTES

Lab Exercise 4.03: Creating and Appending a Text File

Joel wants to create a quiz for his English students. He would like to use the visual editor to create and save the file. Joel wants to be able to add and delete certain lines of text at a later date. He also wants to be able to adjust the screen's display of text to suit his needs. Joel has asked you to help familiarize him with the append mode of the visual editor.

Learning Objectives

In this exercise, you create and append a text file with the visual editor. After you complete this lab, you will be able to:

- Create a text file with the visual editor

- Add and edit text in append mode

- Adjust the screen's display of text

Lab Materials and Setup

For this lab exercise, you'll need:

- Computer with Red Hat Linux 7.3 installed

- Pencil and paper

Getting Down to Business

The following steps guide you in creating a text file with the visual editor in append mode. You will have to apply the knowledge that you acquired in the *Introduction to UNIX and Linux* textbook by John Muster (McGraw-Hill/Osborne, 2002) for appending a text file.

Step 1   Log on to the Linux computer with your username and password. Open a terminal window.

Step 2   Create a new file named *Quiz* with the visual editor. Instruct the editor to move to append mode.

Step 3   Add the following text to the Quiz file:

Quiz

Fill in the blank with the appropriate answer.

1. I think _____ the best student in the class!

a) you're

b) your

2. _____ book is this?

a) Who's

b) Whose

3. _____ boyfriend is handsome.

a) Your

b) You're

4. I like ice cream _____

a) two

b) too

5. The _____ is rainy and cold today.

a) whether

b) weather

Step 4   Inform the visual editor that you want to return to command mode. Save the Quiz file and quit the visual editor. Open the Quiz file in the shell with **more** Quiz to verify that your input was saved correctly.

Step 5   Reopen the Quiz file with the visual editor. Instruct the visual editor to move to append mode.

Step 6   Add the following text to the end of the Quiz file:

6. Sasha the dog knows _____ name.

a) its

b) it's

What two commands instruct the editor to add text at the cursor position in append mode? Briefly describe and compare each command.

_____

_____

Step 7   Instruct the visual editor to switch to command mode and to move your cursor at a line near the midpoint of the screen. Open a new line above where the cursor is located and insert the following text:

(The following questions are worth 5 points each.)

Step 8   Adjust the screen's display of text by issuing the command to scroll down one screen of text in the file. Save and exit the _Quiz_ file with the new changes. Log off the computer.

 15 MINUTES

Lab Exercise 4.04: Issuing Instructions to the Shell and Visual Editor

Joel wants to create a script with the visual editor, but he is unsure of how to accomplish this. He is familiar with adding and deleting text through the append mode of the editor, but has asked for your help in understanding how commands and text can be issued together through the visual editor to create a script.

Learning Objectives

In this exercise, you create a script and issue instructions to the shell and visual editor. After you complete this lab, you will be able to:

- Differentiate between instructions to the shell and the visual editor

- Create a script file using the visual editor

- Execute a script

Lab Materials and Setup

For this lab exercise, you'll need:

- Computer with Red Hat Linux 7.3 installed

- Pencil and paper

Getting Down to Business

The following steps guide you in creating a script with the visual editor. You will have to apply the knowledge that you acquired in the *Introduction to UNIX and Linux* textbook by John Muster (McGraw-Hill/Osborne, 2002) for issuing instructions to the shell and the visual editor.

Step 1   Log on to the Linux computer with your username and password. Open a terminal window.

Step 2   Begin the process of creating a new script called *Users* through the visual editor. Instruct the editor to move to append mode and add the following lines of text:

echo *The date today is*

date

echo *The following users are currently logged on*

who

Instruct the editor that you want to stop adding text, save the script, and exit the visual editor.

Step 3   At the shell prompt, execute the **date** and **who** commands. How does the output of the commands in the shell differ from the result of typing the commands in the append mode of the visual editor?

_____

_____

Step 4   Make the *Users* script executable by executing the **chmod +x** *Users* command. Execute the script. How does the result of executing the script compare with the execution of the **date** and **who** commands in the shell? Log off the computer.

_____

_____

 30 MINUTES

Lab Exercise 4.05: Making Text Changes

Joel wants to edit the new *Users* script he created to add and edit text. He wants to save several versions of the text he is about to add to the script in different script files. He wants to complete all of the changes as quickly as possible, using the advanced commands for making text changes in the visual editor.

Learning Objectives

In this exercise, you work with the visual editor to make text changes. After you complete this lab, you will be able to:

- Copy and paste text
- Search for and substitute text
- Replace and move characters and words

Lab Materials and Setup

For this lab exercise, you'll need:

- Computer with Red Hat Linux 7.3 installed
- Pencil and paper

Getting Down to Business

The following steps guide you in making changes to a text file with the visual editor. You will have to apply the knowledge that you acquired in the *Introduction to UNIX and Linux* textbook by John Muster (McGraw-Hill/Osborne, 2002) for deleting, copying, moving, and replacing text.

Step 1 Log on to the Linux computer with your username and password. Open a terminal window.

Step 2 Open the *Users* script with the visual editor in append mode. Add the following text to the end of the *Users* script:

echo *A. UNIVERSITY POLICY*

IMPORTANT

1. All courses and instructors are to be evaluated by students each semester.

2. Results of the evaluations are to be communicated quarterly to faculty members.

3. Student evaluations are to be taken into account in the annual departmental evaluations of the faculty, and in consideration of cases for promotion and tenure.

Step 3   Using the **forward search** command, switch to command mode and move the cursor to the word *quarterly*. Replace the word *quarterly* with the word *monthly*. What command can be used to accomplish the word replacement?

_____

_____

Step 4   Replace the text *faculty members.* with *department heads.* on the current line of text.

Step 5   Copy and paste the text *A. IMPORTANT* from its current location to the end of the last line of the script. What commands can be executed to accomplish this task?

_____

_____

Step 6   Search for the first occurrence of the word *annual* and substitute with the word *yearly* for the current text.

Step 7   Save this modified version of the *Users* script to a file named *Users2*. Exit the original version of the *Users* script without saving the new changes.

Step 8   Open the *Users2* script and verify that the changes you made have been saved. Using the **write** command, write the last three lines of the *Users2* script to a new file named *Users3*.

Step 9   Exit the visual editor and return to the shell. Open the *Users3* file and verify that it has been created successfully. Exit the shell and log off the computer.

Lab Analysis Test

1. Why is the visual editor such an essential tool? Give three reasons.

_____

_____

2. What functions are available to a user when operating in command mode of the visual editor?

_____

_____

3. What is the difference between cursor-positioning commands and display-adjusting commands?

_____

_____

4. What type of commands begin with a colon and require an ENTER in order for them to be started in the visual editor?

_____

_____

5. What is the correct syntax of the **substitute** command and what is its function in the visual editor?

_____

_____

Key Term Quiz

Use the following vocabulary terms to complete the sentences below. Not all of the terms will be used.

append mode

augmented direction commands

b

command mode

cw

dd

dw

:set nonumber

:set number

u

:q

w

:wq

x

yy

1. The _____ command deletes the current word and places it in the memory buffer.

2. You can instruct the visual editor to display line numbers with the _____ command.

3. The _____ command copies or yanks the current line into memory buffer.

4. To change one word in a sentence into another word in the visual editor, you can use the _____ command.

5. To quit a file without saving the changes, you can execute the _____ command.

Lab Wrap-Up

You should now be familiar with using the visual editor in command mode and append mode. As you have seen, the visual editor allows you to create text by giving all instructions through combinations of keystrokes as well as allowing you to enter text directly to a file. The visual editor also has allowed you to access files, navigate through lines of text, and edit the content within files. You should have successfully created files and script, and familiarized yourself with the several useful editing commands.

Solutions

In this section, you'll find solutions to the Lab Exercises.

Lab Solution 4.01

The following steps should help Sam in editing his *Novel* file with the visual editor in command mode:

Step 1   You should have successfully logged on to the Linux computer with your username and password and opened a terminal window.

Step 2   To ensure that you have the *Novel* file in your home directory, you should have listed the contents of the directory by issuing the **ls** command to the shell. The **more** *Novel* command instructs the shell to open the *Novel* file so you can view the contents.

Step 3   Once you have viewed the contents of the file with the shell, you should have opened the *Novel* file with the visual editor by issuing the **vi** *Novel* command. The contents of the file should appear to be exactly the same as when opened by the shell, indicated in Figure 4-1.

Step 4   You should have navigated through the *Novel* file by using either the **j** or ↓ direction key. Each of these two keys moves the cursor down one line at a time.

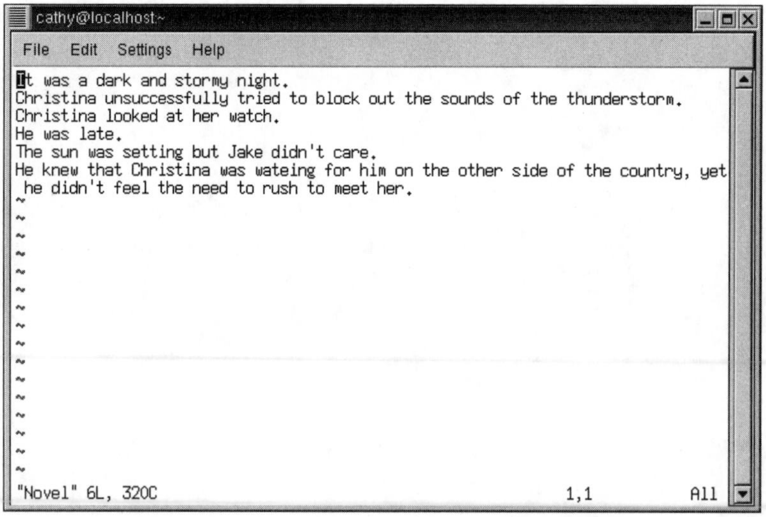

FIGURE 4-1 Viewing the *Novel* file in the visual editor

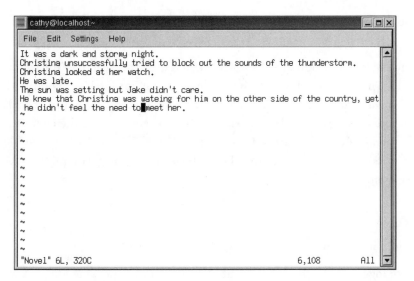

FIGURE 4-2 Edited text shown in the visual editor

Step 5 To navigate in each direction through the file, the following direction keys are available to you: **h** (left), **j** (down), **k** (up), **l** (right), and ←, ↑, →, ↓.

Step 6 The **/the** command instructs the visual editor to search through the *Novel* file, and locate and move the cursor to the word *the*. Once you had located the first occurrence of the word *the*, you should have used the **n** command to indicate that you would like to locate the next *the* and every other occurrence thereafter. By executing the command over and over again, each instance of the word *the* will be located.

Step 7 You should have entered the command **/rush**, which instructs the visual editor to search through the *Novel* file, and locate and move the cursor to the word *rush*. To instruct the **vi** editor to delete the words *rush to*, you should have moved the cursor over each letter (and space) and pressed the **x** key to delete the character. You should have been left with the following sentence, as shown in Figure 4-2:

> He knew that Christina was wateing for him on the other side of the country,
> yet he didn't feel the need to meet her

Step 8 You should have used the arrow or direction keys to navigate to the first line of text in the *Novel* file. You should have then instructed the editor to delete the entire line of text by moving your cursor to the middle of the line and issuing the **dd** (drop dead) command. The entire line of text should have been deleted. In order to undo the deletion of the text, you should have executed the **u** command, which tells the **vi** editor to go back and undo the previous change.

Step 9   You should have saved your edits to the *Novel* file and quit the visual editor by executing the **:wq** command. This command writes the file back to the hard drive and quits the **vi** program. You should have confirmed that you have exited the **vi** editor by issuing the **dir** command, which communicates directly with the shell to list the contents of the current directory. Opening the *Novel* file with the **more** *Novel* command enables you to view the file and confirm that your edits have been saved. You should have successfully completed the lab and logged off the computer.

Lab Solution 4.02

The following steps should help Sam navigate through his *Novel* text file:

Step 1   You should have logged on to the Linux computer with your username and password and opened a terminal window.

Step 2   You should have opened the *Novel* text file with the visual editor by executing the **vi** *Novel* command. In order to implement the use of augmented direction keys to navigate through the file, you should have issued the following commands:

    a)   Move four lines down: **4↓** or **4j**

    b)   Move 6 spaces right: **6→** or **6l**

    c)   Move 2 lines up: **2↑** or **2k**

    d)   Move 4 spaces left: **4←** or **4h**

    Your final location in the text should have been the third character in the third line as shown in Figure 4-3.

Step 3   To display the line numbers, for each line of text in the *Novel* file, you should have executed the command **:set number**, as shown in Figure 4-4. The command to turn off line numbers would be **:set nonumber**.

Step 4   To instruct the visual editor to go to the following specific lines of the *Novel* file, you should have indicated the following commands:

    a)   Fourth line of the file: **4G** or **:8**

    b)   Last line of the file: **G** or **:$**

    c)   Line 2: **2G** or **:2**

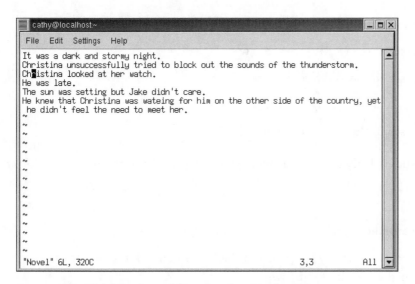

FIGURE 4-3 Final navigated location in visual editor

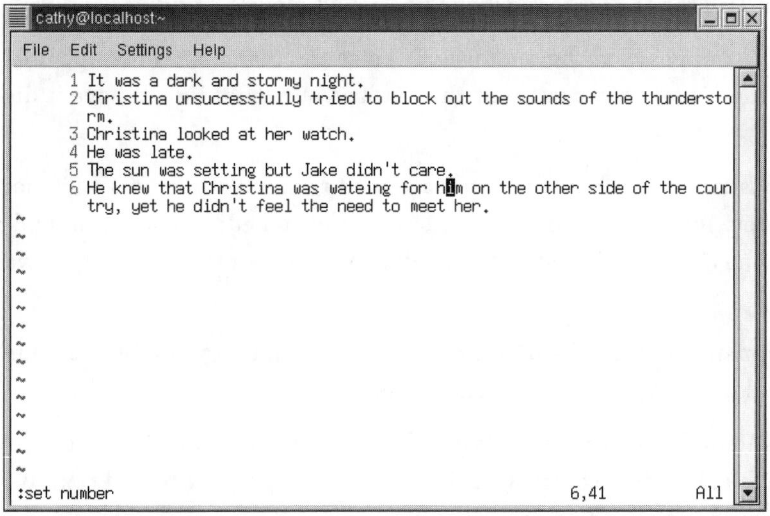

FIGURE 4-4 Viewing the line numbers in visual editor

Step 5 To search through the *Novel* file according to the following instructions, you should have indicated the following commands:

a) 2 lines down from current location: **2↓** or **2j**

b) Search for the letter *e*: **/e**

c)   Search backward through the file for the previous occurrence of the letter *e*: **?e**

d)   Move the cursor three words forward: **3w**

e)   Move the cursor to the end of the current line: **$**

f)   Position the cursor at the highest line on the screen: **H**

g)   Move the cursor to the last line of the file: **:$**

You should have successfully completed the lab and logged off the computer.

Lab Solution 4.03

The following steps should help Joel create and append a *Quiz* text file:

Step 1   You should have successfully logged on to the Linux computer with your username and password and opened a terminal window.

Step 2   To create a new file named *Quiz* with the visual editor, you should have executed the **vi** *Quiz* command, and instructed the editor to move to append mode by typing **a**.

Step 3   You should have simply typed the text as written to the *Quiz* file, as the append mode allows you to use the visual editor to input the text as you would like to have it displayed.

Step 4   To inform the visual editor that you want to return to command mode, you should have pressed the ESCAPE key. To save the *Quiz* file and quit the visual editor, the command **:wq** should have been used. The *Quiz* file viewed in the shell should verify that your input was saved correctly.

Step 5   The **vi** *Quiz* command reopens the *Quiz* file with the visual editor, and the **a** command instructs the visual editor to move to append mode.

Step 6   The new text should have been typed directly after the last line of the current *Quiz* file, extending the file. The two commands that instruct the editor to add text at the cursor position in append mode are the **a** and **i** commands. Both commands move you from command mode to append mode; however, every character you type after the **i** command is entered as text in your file starting to the left of the cursor. With the **a** command, the text is entered to the right of the cursor position.

Step 7   You should have instructed the visual editor to switch to command mode by using the ESCAPE key and to move your cursor at a line near the midpoint of the screen by issuing the **M** command. To then open a new line above where the cursor is located, the **O** command should have been used. At this point you should have inserted the text (*The following questions are worth 5 points each.*).

Step 8   To adjust the screen's display of text, you should have issued the CTRL-D command to scroll down one screen of text in the file. You should have once again saved and exited the *Quiz* file using the **:wq** command and logged off the computer.

Lab Solution 4.04

The following steps should guide you in issuing instructions to the shell and visual editor:

Step 1   You should have successfully logged on to the Linux computer with your username and password and opened a terminal window.

Step 2   To begin the process of creating a new script called *Users* through the visual editor, you should have executed the **vi** *Users* command and instructed the editor to move to append mode by issuing the **a** command. You should have then added the indicated lines of text. Instructing the editor to stop adding text requires that you use the CTRL-D command. You should have saved the script and exited the visual editor with the **:wq** command.

Step 3   After executing the **date** and **who** commands, the output of each command shows the current date and the users who are currently logged on. Typing the **date** and **who** commands in the append mode of the visual editor does not result in the output of each utility. They are simply two typed words in a text file script. It is only after executing the script that the output from each command is produced.

Step 4   You should have made the *Users* script executable by executing the **chmod +x** *Users* command and executed the script by typing **./***Users*. The result of executing the script should be similar to the execution of the **date** and **who** commands in the shell. The script runs both commands and displays the output of the utilities on the screen, as shown in Figure 4-5. The output appears along with the echoed text from the script. You should have successfully completed the lab and logged off the computer.

```
 ▤ cathy@h24-70-178-84:~                                    _ □ ✕

  File   Edit   Settings   Help

 [cathy@h24-70-178-84 cathy]$ ./Users                        ▲
 The date today is
 Sat Aug 31 01:11:24 CDT 2002
 The following users are currently logged on
 cathy    pts/0    Aug 31 01:11 (:0)
 [cathy@h24-70-178-84 cathy]$ date
 Sat Aug 31 01:11:31 CDT 2002
 [cathy@h24-70-178-84 cathy]$ who
 cathy    pts/0    Aug 31 01:11 (:0)
 [cathy@h24-70-178-84 cathy]$ ▮

                                                            ▼
```

FIGURE 4-5 The *Users* script outputs the executed commands

Lab Solution 4.05

The following steps should guide you in making text changes:

Step 1   You should have successfully logged on to the Linux computer with your username and password and opened a terminal window.

Step 2   To open the *Users* script with the visual editor in append mode you should have typed **vi** *Users* and then issued the **a** command to move to append mode. To add the text to the end of the *Users* script you should have scrolled down to the end of the text, and simply typed the text as written.

Step 3   In order to switch to command mode, and search for and move your cursor to the word *quarterly*, you should have executed the command **/quarterly**. To replace the word *quarterly* with the word *monthly*, you should have issued the **cw** command and typed the word *monthly*.

Step 4   To replace the text *faculty members.* with *department heads.*, you should have scrolled to the space before the text, ensured that you are in command mode, and typed the command **C** to change the text and then typed the new text *department heads.*.

Step 5   To copy and paste the text *A. IMPORTANT* from its current location to the end of the last line of the script, you should have scrolled to the text itself, and in command mode executed the command **yy**, which copies the entire line of text into the buffer. Then you should have scrolled down to the new location at the end of the last line and executed the **p** command, which pastes the text from the buffer to the file.

Step 6   To search for the first occurrence of the word *annual*, you should have executed the */annual* command. To substitute the word *yearly* for the current text, you should have typed the command **:s/annual/yearly/**.

Step 7   You should have saved this modified version of the *Users* script to a file named *Users2* by executing the **:w** *Users2* command. To exit the original version of the *Users* script without saving the new changes, you should have executed the **:q** command.

Step 8   To open the *Users2* script and verify that the changes you made have been saved, you should have executed the **vi** *Users2* command. To use the **write** command to write the last three lines of the *Users2* script to a new file named *Users3*, you would first have to display the line numbers of the script using the **:set number** command. Once the numbers are displayed, you could then write the last three lines to the new script by executing the command **:8, 10 write** *Users3*.

Step 9   You should have exited the visual editor with the **:wq** command and returned to the shell. To open the *Users3* file and verify that it has been created successfully, you should have typed **vi** *Users3*. You should have exited the shell, successfully completed the lab, and logged off the computer.

Chapter 5

Using Basic Linux and UNIX Utilities

Lab Exercises

So far in this lab manual, you have been introduced to the various utility programs of UNIX/Linux. You have briefly explored utilities that locate system information, sort lines, select specific fields, modify information, and manage files for users. This chapter delves into the advanced features of each utility and explores how these programs can aid you in your everyday tasks of collecting, modifying, and storing data.

This chapter also examines how you can use several utilities in combination to manipulate and compare data, perform mathematical calculations, and search and sort through files. You will create files, select a portion of each line in a file, concatenate files, and splice lines of data together. Finally, you will output the results of employing these utilities to other utilities and files and keep track of when modifications were made to files.

 20 MINUTES

Lab Exercise 5.01: Counting Elements in a File

Katherine has created a text file named *Canada* that contains information on how to obtain a Canadian work visa. She wants to count the number of lines in the *Canada* file and save the results to a separate file named *LineCount* to present the results to her boss. Once she has created the new file, she would like to combine it with the original *Canada* file for her own viewing. She also wants a total word count for all files in her home directory.

Learning Objectives

In this lab, you count the words, lines, and characters in a file. By the end of this lab, you'll be able to:

- Count words in all files of a directory

- Count words, lines, and characters in a file

- Count elements in the output of a utility

- Merge and examine file content

Lab Materials and Setup

The materials you need for this lab are:

- Computer with Red Hat Linux 7.3 installed

- Pencil and paper

Getting Down to Business

The following steps guide you in counting file elements. You will also have to apply the knowledge that you acquired in the *Introduction to UNIX and Linux* textbook by John Muster (McGraw-Hill/Osborne, 2002) for examining and merging files.

Step 1 Log on to the Linux computer with your username and password. Open a terminal window.

Step 2 At your home directory, issue the command that counts the number of words for each file in your current directory. Record the command and the result in the space provided.

_____

_____

Step 3 Create a file in your home directory named *Canada* with the contents shown in Figure 5-1.

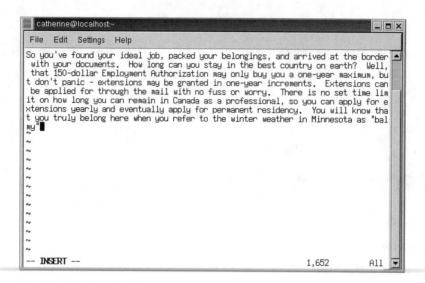

FIGURE 5-1 *Canada* file contents

Step 4 Execute the command to count the number of words for each file in your current directory. Has the word count been updated to include the *Canada* file? Execute a single command to count the number of words and characters in the *Canada* text file. Record your results in the space provided.

_____

_____

Step 5 Execute an additional single command that produces the same output (number of words and characters). How does this command differ from the first command you executed? Why do both commands produce the same output?

_____

_____

Step 6 Execute a command that counts the words in the output from the list of files in the current directory. Explain how the word count is generated when using this type of command.

_____

_____

Step 7 Count the number of lines in the *Canada* file and save the output to a file named *LineCount* in your home directory. View the contents of the *LineCount* file to verify it was created successfully.

Step 8 Create a file named *CanadaInfo* that combines the output of both the *Canada* and *LineCount* files. Open and view the *CanadaInfo* file, displaying line numbers on each line of the merged file. Does the *CanadaInfo* file show the results of the merged *Canada* and *LineCount* files?

_____

_____

Step 9 Open the *CanadaInfo* file in the visual editor and copy six lines of text from the beginning of the *CanadaInfo* file and paste it to the end of the file. Repeat this process three additional times. Save and exit the file.

Step 10 View the contents of the *CanadaInfo* file by using the **more** utility. Scroll through the file by using the ENTER key and SPACEBAR. How do the results of using each key differ when scrolling through the file? Exit the terminal and log off the computer.

_____

_____

 30 MINUTES

Lab Exercise 5.02: Employing Search Utilities

Katherine wants to search through her *Canada* text file for specific character strings. She does not want to have to look at every word in the file in order to find what she's looking for. She has asked for your help in searching through the file for all words that contain the characters *can*. She is also interested in rejecting any line of text that contains the word *Canada*. She wants several additional searches completed on the *Canada* file, as well as other files, and has asked for your guidance.

Learning Objectives

In this lab exercise, you employ the **grep** utility to search through files for a target string of characters. After you complete this lab, you will be able to:

- Search for a target string of characters
- Search multiple files
- Search for multiple-word targets

Lab Materials and Setup

For this lab exercise, you'll need:

- Computer with Red Hat Linux 7.3 installed
- Pencil and paper
- Successful completion of Lab 5.01

Getting Down to Business

The following steps guide you in searching through a file with the **grep** utility. You will have to apply the knowledge that you acquired in the *Introduction to UNIX and Linux* textbook by John Muster (McGraw-Hill/Osborne, 2002) for searching multiple files for multiple-word targets.

Step 1   Log on to the Linux computer with your username and password. Open a terminal window.

Step 2   Search the *Canada* file for the following target strings:

a)   All lines that contain the string *can*.

b)   All lines that do not contain the string *Canada*.

c)   All lines that contain the string *can*, ignoring the case.

d)   All lines that contain the string *can you*.

e)   All lines that contain three-character words that start with the letter *c* and end with the letter *n*.

f)   All lines that start with the letter *s*.

g)   All lines that end with the letter *t*.

Record the commands you executed to obtain your results in the space provided.

_____

_____

Step 3   How does searching for the string *can* differ from searching for the string *c.n*? Are the results different? Why or why not?

_____

_____

Step 4   Create a file named *America* with the text shown in Figure 5-2.

Step 5   Search both the *Canada* and *America* files for the target string *bor*. Record your results in the space provided.

_____

_____

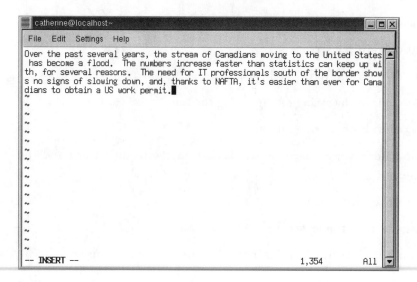

FIGURE 5-2 *America* file contents

Step 6   Search all files in your home directory for the target string *th* and list only the file-names that contain the string. Record your results in the space provided.

_____

_____

Step 7   Search the *Canada* and *America* files for any word that contains the characters *ou*, list-ing the line numbers for each target match in the output. Record your results in the space provided. Log off the computer.

_____

_____

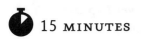 15 MINUTES

Lab Exercise 5.03: Performing Math Calculations

Natalie wants to calculate her earnings to see if she has enough money to take a vacation to Hawaii. She is unsure of how to use the calculator in Linux and has asked for your help in performing basic math calculations. She has provided you with a list of her earnings and expenses, as well as the costs of travel to Hawaii.

Learning Objectives

In this exercise, you perform basic math calculations with the **bc** utility. After you complete this lab, you will be able to:

- Perform basic math calculations
- Use floating-point operations
- Identify order of operations

Lab Materials and Setup

For this lab exercise, you'll need:

- Computer with Red Hat Linux 7.3 installed
- Pencil and paper

Getting Down to Business

The following steps guide you in performing several math calculations. You will have to apply the knowledge that you acquired in the *Introduction to UNIX and Linux* textbook by John Muster (McGraw-Hill/Osborne, 2002) for using the **bc** utility and **scale** command.

Step 1   Log on to the Linux computer with your username and password. Open a terminal window.

Step 2   At the terminal window, call up the calculator utility. Complete the following calculations based on the information provided on the following page.

Earnings	Expenses	Travel Expenses
$3000/month for 6 months	Housing: $2200/month for 6 months	Airfare: $850.48
$4000 advance on book deal	Utilities: $65/month for 6 months	Hotel: $1306.10
$2200.58 royalties	Food and entertainment: $1000/month for 6 months	Food and entertainment: $1500
	Misc. bills: $100/month for 6 months	Tips and misc.: $200

a)   Natalie's total earnings

b)   Natalie's total expenses

c)   Total travel expenses

d)   Available net earnings

Ensure that your results are of two-decimal place accuracy. Note the results for each calculation in the space provided.

_____

_____

Step 3   Does Natalie have enough money to pay for her vacation to Hawaii? What was the order of operations when calculating her total earnings and expenses? Log off the computer.

_____

_____

 30 MINUTES

Lab Exercise 5.04: Sorting Through Files

Christy works at the Department of Motor Vehicles and is responsible for keeping track of license plate records. She wants to know how she can easily sort through several files to organize the user and plate data she has input to her Linux computer. She also wants to identify unique lines and compare data.

Learning Objectives

In this exercise, you order the lines of a file by using the **sort** utility. After you complete this lab, you will be able to:

- Sort a file in dictionary order

- Sort by numerical value and fields

- Compare and identify unique data

Lab Materials and Setup

For this lab exercise, you'll need:

- Computer with Red Hat Linux 7.3 installed

- Pencil and paper

Getting Down to Business

The following steps guide you in sorting the lines of a file. You will have to apply the knowledge that you acquired in the *Introduction to UNIX and Linux* textbook by John Muster (McGraw-Hill/Osborne, 2002) for sorting the elements of a file based on several different criteria.

Step 1 Log on to the Linux computer with your username and password. Open a terminal window.

Step 2 Create a file named *Plates* with the data shown in Figure 5-3.

```
┌─ catherine@localhost:~ ──────────────────────────── _ □ ✕ ─┐
│ File  Edit  Settings  Help                                 │
│ RVX790  Susan    Jaimeson   A.                         ▲   │
│ 450TGH  Keith    Mcpherson  F.                             │
│ SPEEDY  Janice   Stevenson  G.                             │
│ AMEN!   Linda    Williams   S.                             │
│ _55MPH  John     Thompson   J.                             │
│ ?WhoMe? William  Stevenson  K.                             │
│ +WWW    Kenneth  Simonson   T.                             │
│ 39FINE  Mario    Tenentes   C.                             │
│ █                                                          │
│ ~                                                          │
│ ~                                                          │
│ ~                                                          │
│ ~                                                          │
│ ~                                                          │
│ ~                                                          │
│ ~                                                          │
│ ~                                                          │
│ ~                                                          │
│ ~                                                          │
│ ~                                                          │
│ ~                                                          │
│ "Plates" 9L, 206C                    9,0-1          All ▼  │
└────────────────────────────────────────────────────────────┘
```

Figure 5-3 *Plates* file contents

Step 3 Sort the *Plates* file according to the following criteria:

a) Dictionary order, ignoring the case

b) Numerical order

c) Last name

Record the commands you used to sort the file in the space provided.

_____

_____

Step 4 Redirect the output of the last-name sort (Step 3c) to a file named *SecondSort*.

Step 5 Create a data file named *Records* with the following contents:

State	City	Records
AL	Birmingham	5001
DE	Wilmington	5007
AK	Anchorage	5000

State	City	Records
CT	Hartford	5006
AZ	Scottsdale	5002
GA	Savannah	5009
AR	Little Rock	5003
CO	Fort Collins	5005
CO	Fort Collins	5005
FL	Tampa Bay	5008
CA	Los Angeles	5004
DE	Wilmington	5007
HI	Honolulu	5010

Step 6 Sort the *Records* file so that all duplicate lines are removed from the file and only unique lines are displayed in the output. Direct the output of the sort to a file named *States*. View the *States* file to verify that it was created successfully.

Step 7 Identify the common and unique lines of data in the *Records* and *States* files and direct the output to a new file named *StateRecords*. View the *StateRecords* file and identify the unique lines of data. Log off the computer.

 30 MINUTES

Lab Exercise 5.05: Modifying and Manipulating Data

Krystin is trying to keep track of the groceries and prices in her Italian food store. She wants to learn how to quickly modify and manipulate data in her *Groceries* file by using several utilities. She has asked for your help in completing several simple tasks.

Learning Objectives

In this exercise, you modify and manipulate data by employing the **cut**, **paste**, **sed**, and **awk** utilities. After you complete this lab you will be able to:

- Cut and paste data in a file

- Modify data with the **sed** utility

- Manipulate data with the **awk** utility

Lab Materials and Setup

For this lab exercise, you'll need:

- Computer with Red Hat Linux 7.3 installed

- Pencil and paper

Getting Down to Business

The following steps guide you in stream editing with the **sed** utility and manipulating data with the **cut**, **paste**, and **awk** utilities. You will have to apply the knowledge that you acquired in the *Introduction to UNIX and Linux* textbook by John Muster (McGraw-Hill/Osborne, 2002) for selecting and replacing data with all utilities.

Step 1   Log on to the Linux computer with your username and password. Open a terminal window.

Step 2   Create a file named *Groceries* with the contents indicated in Figure 5-4.

```
catherine@localhost:~

 File  Edit  Settings  Help

Milk low-fat skim $4.00
Apples green pear $3.00 apples apples apples
Cheese feta cheddar $6.00
Coffee decaf instant $5.00
█
~
~
~
~
~
~
~
~
~
~
~
~
~
~
~
~
~
~
"Groceries" 5L, 123C                          5,0-1        All
```

FIGURE 5-4 *Groceries* file contents

Step 3 In the *Groceries* file, attempt to replace every instance of the word *apples* with the word *oranges* using the stream editor. Does the editor successfully replace every instance of the word *apples*? Why or why not?

_____

_____

Step 4 Delete the entire *coffee* line with the stream editor.

Step 5 Instruct the **awk** utility to print the fourth field from the *cheese* line to the screen. What is the output?

_____

_____

Step 6 Edit the *Groceries* file by cutting the first field of each line of the file. What is the output?

_____

_____

Step 7 Splice the lines of the *Groceries* file together using the **paste** utility. Ensure that the space character is used as the separator in the output. Log off the computer.

Lab Analysis Test

1. How can you use the **grep** utility to search through a file but reject all target-matching lines, and output only non-matching lines?

_____

_____

2. What does the command **sort +2 -3 +1 -2 _filename_** accomplish?

_____

_____

3. What is the function of the **tee** utility?

_____

_____

4. How can using the **sed** utility provide advantages over the **vi** utility when editing a file?

_____

_____

5. What are the main functions of the **awk** utility?

_____

_____

Key Term Quiz

Use the following vocabulary terms to complete the sentences below. Not all of the terms will be used.

    awk

    bc

    column

    comm.

    grep

    sed

    sort

    tee

    touch

    tr

    uniq

    wc

1. An editor that reads in individual lines and works on streams of data is known as _____.

2. The _____ utility is designed to locate records and fields in a database, modify them, perform computations, and then output selected portions of the data.

3. You can use the _____ utility to identify which of many files contains a specific string of characters.

4. The _____ utility can be used to compare files line by line.

5. You can use the _____ utility to search through every character in a file and delete specific characters.

Lab Wrap-Up

You should now be familiar with a variety of UNIX utilities. You should have successfully employed several utilities with their associated options. With these utilities, you searched, sorted, modified, combined, calculated, and compared data and output results.

Solutions

In this section, you'll find solutions to the Lab Exercises.

Lab Solution 5.01

The following steps should guide you in counting the elements in Katherine's files and directory:

Step 1 You should have successfully logged on to the Linux computer with your username and password and opened a terminal window.

Step 2 At your home directory, you should have issued the **wc** * command, which counts the number of lines, words, and characters for each file in your current directory and displays a total for each category. The result of the word count may vary depending on what files you currently have in your home directory.

Step 3 You should have opened the visual editor, **pico** editor, or issued the **cat** *Canada* command to create a file in your home directory named *Canada* with the indicated contents.

Step 4 You should have executed the **wc** * command to count the number of words for each file in your current directory. The result should have indicated an updated number of words to include the word count from the *Canada* file. A command that would successfully count the number of words and characters in the *Canada* text file would be **wc -wc** *Canada*. This command presents the arguments **-w** (words) and **-c** (characters) as a combined option. The result should have been 113 words with 653 characters.

Step 5 An additional command that produces the same output (number of words and characters) as the **wc -wc** *Canada* command executed in Step 4, would be the **wc -cw** *Canada* command. The order of the arguments in the command have been reversed, but the output for the command would be the same as the words and characters of the *Canada* file that are counted regardless of what order the arguments are presented.

Step 6 You should have executed the **ls | wc** command. This command counts the words in the output from the list of files in the current directory. The word count is generated from the output of the **ls** utility. First, the utility lists all files in the current directory. Then the listed output is piped to the **wc** utility for further processing. The **wc** utility counts the lines, words, and characters that comprise the list. The **wc** utility does not read and count the contents of each listed file. It simply reads the list of files and generates a count from the list.

Step 7 You should have counted the number of lines in the *Canada* file and saved the output to a file named *LineCount* in your home directory by executing the command **wc -l** *Canada* > *LineCount*. To view the contents of the *LineCount* file, you should have executed the command **cat** *LineCount*.

Step 8   To create a file named *CanadaInfo* that combines the output of both the *Canada* and *LineCount* files, you should have executed the command **cat** *Canada LineCount* **>** *CanadaInfo*. To open and view the *CanadaInfo* file, displaying line numbers on each line of the merged file, you should have executed the command **cat -n** *CanadaInfo*. The *CanadaInfo* file should show the results of the merged *Canada* and *LineCount* files.

Step 9   To open the *CanadaInfo* file in the visual editor and copy six lines of text from the beginning of the *CanadaInfo* file and paste it to the end of the file, you should have completed the following steps:

vi CanadaInfo

6yy

:$

ENTER

$

P

   You should have repeated the last four lines of the above code three additional times and then typed **:wq** to save and exit the file.

Step 10   To view the contents of the *CanadaInfo* file by using the **more** utility, you should have typed **more** *CanadaInfo*. You should have then scrolled through the file by using the ENTER key and SPACEBAR. The ENTER key is an instruction to add the next single line to the display. The SPACEBAR instructs the **more** utility to display the next page of output. You should have successfully completed the lab, exited the terminal, and logged off the computer.

Lab Solution 5.02

The following steps should guide you in helping Katherine search through her files:

Step 1   You should have successfully logged on to the Linux computer with your username and password and opened a terminal window.

Step 2   When searching the *Canada* file for the indicated target strings, you should have executed the following commands:

a)   **grep can** *Canada*

The string *can* is searched for directly.

b) **grep -v** *Canada Canada*

The **-v** option rejects all lines that match the target string and outputs all other lines.

c) **grep -i** *Canada*

The **-i** option tells the **grep** utility to ignore the case while searching for the target string.

d) **grep** *'can you' Canada*

The multiple-word string is contained in quotes to produce the correct result.

e) **grep** *'c.n' Canada*

The *'c.n'* string indicates a three-character string that begins with the letter *c* and ends with the letter *n*.

f) **grep** *'∧s'* **Canada**

The *'∧s'* string indicates a target string that begins with the letter *s*.

g) **grep** *'t$'* **Canada**

The *'t$'* string indicates a line that ends with the letter *t*.

Step 3   Searching for the string *can* differs from searching for the string *c.n* because by issuing the *'c.n'* target, the results could contain all words that contain any character as the middle character, while the *'can'* target specifically searches for the letter *a* as the second character of the string. The results may not be different in this particular *Canada* file, as there may not be words that contain characters other than *can*.

Step 4   You should have successfully created a file named *America* with the indicated text by using the **vi** editor, **pico** editor, or the **cat** *America* command and typing the text.

Step 5   To search both the *Canada* and *America* files for the target string *bor*, you should have executed the command **grep** *bor Canada America* **| more.**

Step 6   To search all files in your home directory for the target string *th* and list only the filenames that contain the string, you should have executed the command **grep -l** *th* *.

Step 7   To search the *Canada* and *America* files for any word that contains the characters **ou**, and listing the line numbers for each target match in the output, you should have executed the command **grep -n** *ou Canada America* **| more.** You should have successfully completed the lab and logged off the computer.

Lab Solution 5.03

The following steps should guide you in calculating Natalie's earnings and expenses:

Step 1   You should have successfully logged on to the Linux computer with your username and password and opened a terminal window.

Step 2   At the terminal window, you should have called up the calculator utility by executing the command **bc**. After completing the calculations based on the information provided, you should have come up with the following results:

   a)   Natalie's total earnings: (3000*6)+4000+2200.58 = 24,200.58

   b)   Natalie's total expenses: (2200*6)+(65*6)+(1000*6)+(100*6)= 20,190.00

   c)   Total travel expenses: 850.48+1306.10+1500+200=3856.58

   d)   Available net earnings: 24,200.58–20,190.00=4010.58

   In order to display all two-decimal place numbers, you may or may not have had to use the command **scale=2** before calculating the equations.

Step 3   You should have determined that Natalie does have enough money to pay for her vacation to Hawaii as her available net earnings calculate to $4010.58 and the total travel expenses for the vacation would only cost $3856.58. The calculator determines that the numbers you include in brackets (any items that need to be multiplied) will be calculated first, and then their results will be entered into the rest of the equation. You should have successfully complete the lab and logged off the computer.

Lab Solution 5.04

The following steps should guide you in sorting through several files:

Step 1   You should have successfully logged on to the Linux computer with your username and password and opened a terminal window.

Step 2   To create a file named *Plates* with the indicated data, you should have executed the command **vi** *Plates* and typed the data using the TAB key to separate the fields into columns.

Step 3   You should have executed the following commands to sort the *Plates* file according to the criteria:

   a)   Dictionary order, ignoring the case: **sort -d -f** *Plates*

   b)   Numerical order: **sort -n** *Plates*

   c)   Last name: **sort -k 3** *Plates*

Step 4   To redirect the output of the last-name sort to a file named *SecondSort*, you should have executed the command **sort -k** 3 *Plates* **-o** *SecondSort*.

Step 5   To create a data file named *Records* with the indicated contents, you should have executed the command **vi** *Records* and inserted the data using the TAB key to separate the fields into columns.

Step 6   To sort the *Records* file and direct the output of the sort to a file named *States*, making sure that all duplicate lines are removed from the file and only unique lines are displayed in the output, you should have executed the command **uniq -u** *Records* **>** *States*.

Step 7   To identify the common and unique lines of data in the *Records* and *States* files and direct the output to a new file named *StateRecords*, you should have executed the command **comm** *Records States* **>** *StateRecords*.

Lab Solution 5.05

The following steps should guide you in modifying and manipulating data:

Step 1   You should have successfully logged on to the Linux computer with your username and password and opened a terminal window.

Step 2   To create a file named *Groceries* with the indicated content, you should have executed the command **vi** *Groceries* and then inserted the text and saved the file.

Step 3   In order to replace every instance of the word *apples* with the word *oranges* in the *Groceries* file using the stream editor, you should have typed the command **sed '**s/*apples*/ *oranges*/**g'** *Groceries*. The editor should have successfully replaced every instance of the word *apples*, as you indicated the **g** option, which tells the **sed** utility to globally affect each line of the file.

Step 4   To delete the entire *coffee* line with the stream editor, you should have executed the command **sed '**/*coffee*/d**'** *Groceries*.

Step 5   In order to instruct the **awk** utility to print the fourth field from the *cheese* line to the screen, you should have executed the command **awk '**/*cheese*/ **{print $4}'** *Groceries*. The output should have been the fourth field, which was $6.00.

Step 6   To edit the *Groceries* file by cutting the first field of each line of the file, you should have executed the command **cut -d -f1** *Groceries*. The output should have been:

```
milk
apples
cheese
coffee
```

Step 7 To splice the lines of the *Groceries* file together using the paste utility, you should have executed the command **paste -s -d' '** *Groceries*. You should have successfully completed the lab and logged off the computer.

Chapter 6

Using Multiple Utilities in Scripts

Lab Exercises

Up until now, you have used utilities to obtain system information. This chapter explores how to create scripts that employ multiple utilities to manipulate and retrieve data. You will also have the opportunity to create a complex word analysis script that can be used to detect errors and analyze the code you have written in a script. You'll remove punctuation, make characters lowercase, and alter the display of output text.

Additionally, you will explore creating, modifying, and viewing information files and directories. This will enable you to organize your files and collect important information about each file.

 15 MINUTES

Lab Exercise 6.01: Employing Utilities to Obtain Information

Dean needs a daily written report of the status of his Linux system. He wants to obtain certain information about users and processes that are only accessible by executing utility commands. He does not want to have to execute these commands daily and has asked you to help him write a script that employs these utilities to obtain the information he needs. He would also like the results of the execution of the script to be saved to a file.

Learning Objectives

In this lab, you create a script that employs several utilities to obtain information. By the end of this lab, you'll be able to:

- Recognize utilities that obtain information
- Employ utilities in a script
- Redirect the output of a script to a file

Lab Materials and Setup

The materials you need for this lab are:

- Computer with Red Hat Linux 7.3 installed
- Pencil and paper

Getting Down to Business

The following steps guide you in employing utilities to obtain information. You will have to apply the knowledge that you acquired in the *Introduction to UNIX and Linux* textbook by John Muster (McGraw-Hill/Osborne, 2002) for creating a script.

Step 1   Log on to the Linux computer with your username and password. Open a terminal window.

Step 2   Open the visual editor and prepare to create a script named *Information*. Add the contents from the following table to the script:

Headings	Utilities
Today's date is:	date
The current users logged on to the system are:	who | grep $USER
My current startup directory is:	pwd
Today's identification information is:	id
The processes running on my system are:	ps

✔ **Hint**

Echo the headings in the script in order to identify the results of the utilities upon execution.

Step 3   Save the script and exit to the shell. Make the script executable and proceed to run the *Information* script. Were you successful in creating and running the script?

_____

_____

Step 4   Redirect the output of the *Information* script to a file named *DailyInfo* that Dean can access daily. Log off the computer.

30 MINUTES

Lab Exercise 6.02: Exploring Directories and Files

Sam has several files in his home directory. He has trouble searching through all the files to find what he needs. He wants to organize all files related to his novel, which he accesses regularly, into a new directory. He also wants to easily identify directories and filenames, as well as identify any file permissions or changes made to the files.

Learning Objectives

In this exercise, you explore directories and files on your Linux computer. After you've completed this lab, you will be able to:

- Create and modify directories

- View directories and files separately

- Identify changes made to files in a directory

Lab Materials and Setup

The materials you need for this lab are:

- Computer with Red Hat Linux 7.3 installed

- Pencil and paper

- Successful completion of all previous labs

Getting Down to Business

The following steps guide you in exploring directories and files. You will have to apply the knowledge that you acquired in the *Introduction to UNIX and Linux* textbook by John Muster (McGraw-Hill/Osborne, 2002) for creating directories and obtaining file information.

Step 1   Log on to the Linux computer with your username and password. Open a terminal window.

Step 2   List the files in your current home directory and identify all files that are related to Sam's novel.

Step 3   Create a new directory called *Novelfiles*. Confirm that the new directory exists in your current directory.

Step 4   Move all files related to Sam's novel to the *Novelfiles* directory by typing **mv** *filename Novelfiles* for each file in that directory you want moved.

Step 5   Change your current directory to the *Novelfiles* directory and confirm your location. Verify that you have moved all files successfully. Return to your home directory.

Step 6   Create a file named *Metadata* that lists information about all files listed in the *Novelfiles* directory.

Step 7   List the contents of your home directory to confirm that you have created the file successfully. View the contents of the *Metadata* file. Are you able to view the permissions on each file? In the space provided, list the type of information that is displayed for each file.

_____

_____

Step 8   Move to your *Novelfiles* directory. Change the permissions on the *Chapter_1* file in the new directory to remove the read permission. Return to your home directory.

Step 9   Create a new file called *Metadata2* that contains information about all the files in the *Novelfiles* directory. Compare the differences between the *Metadata* and *Metadata2* files by using the **comm** utility. List the differences in the space provided. Log off the computer.

_____

_____

 30 MINUTES

Lab Exercise 6.03: Creating a Complex Word Analysis Script

Rolf wants to create a script that will analyze his latest newspaper article about the price of gasoline. He wants the script to sort through the text, give a reading of how many duplicate words exist in the article, and remove the duplicate words. He wants to save the results of this analysis to a separate file for later viewing.

Learning Objectives

In this exercise, you create a complex word analysis script. After you complete this lab, you will be able to:

- Create a long text file
- Remove punctuation and make characters lowercase
- Alter the display of lines

Lab Materials and Setup

For this lab exercise, you'll need:

- Computer with Red Hat Linux 7.3 installed
- Pencil and paper

Getting Down to Business

The following steps guide you in creating a complex word analysis script. You will have to apply the knowledge that you acquired in the *Introduction to UNIX and Linux* textbook by John Muster (McGraw-Hill/Osborne, 2002) for removing punctuation, making all characters lowercase, and sorting and removing lines of text.

Step 1   Log on to the Linux computer with your username and password. Open a terminal window.

Step 2   Create and save a new text file called *Gasoline* that consists of the following content:

Gas prices rose only half a penny a gallon in the past two weeks, continuing an unusual 20-week trend of mostly steady prices.

The average price for gas nationwide, including all grades and taxes, was about $1.46 a gallon on Friday, according to a survey of 8,000 stations released Sunday. That was up .5 cents per gallon from Aug. 9. Prices have shown little change since early April, when a gallon of gas also cost about $1.46.

Step 3 Create an analysis script called *TestScript* that completes the following tasks for the *Gasoline* file:

    a) Remove punctuation

    b) Make all characters lowercase

    c) Put each word on a single line

    d) Remove blank lines

    e) Sort the text to put all lines containing the same word on adjacent lines

    f) Remove duplicate words from the text

    g) List most-used words in the file first

    h) Send the output of this script to a file named *ScriptResult*

Step 4 Verify that the script was created successfully. Make the *TestScript* executable. Run the script.

Step 5 Open the *ScriptResult* file and verify that the contents match what was asked for in the *TestScript* script. Log off the computer.

Lab Analysis Test

1. What is the name of the utility in UNIX that lists the unique words used in a file?

_____

_____

2. What is the purpose of creating a word analysis script?

_____

_____

3. In order to properly remove duplicate words, what requirements must be met?

_____

_____

4. What is the **-F** argument used for when combined with the **ls** utility?

_____

_____

5. What is the function of the **tr** utility?

_____

_____

Key Term Quiz

Use the following vocabulary terms to complete the sentences below. Not all of the terms will be used.

awk

column

comm

sed

sort

tee

tr

uniq

wc

1. The _____ utility locates target characters and replaces them with other characters.

2. The difference between two separate snapshot files can be identified by using the _____ utility.

3. The _____ utility deletes a line only if it is adjacent to another identical line.

4. The _____ utility is a stream editor that takes text on its input stream, makes the specified changes, and sends the modified text to the output stream.

5. A _____ allows you to take the output from a command and direct it into a file and to another command.

Lab Wrap-Up

You should now be familiar with creating scripts that employ multiple utilities to manipulate and retrieve data. You should have successfully created a complex word analysis script and analyzed the code you had written in a script. Additionally, you explored creating, modifying, and viewing files and directories. You should now be comfortable with how to organize your files, collect important information about each file, and create and analyze effective scripts.

Solutions

In this section, you'll find solutions to the Lab Exercises.

Lab Solution 6.01

The following steps should guide you in employing utilities to obtain information:

Step 1 You should have logged on to the Linux computer with your username and password and opened a terminal window.

Step 2 To open the visual editor and create a script named *Information*, you should have executed the **vi** *Information* command and then switched from command mode to append mode by typing the **a** command. When adding the content from the table to the script, the resulting script would be:

> **echo** *The date today is*
>
> **date**
>
> **echo** *The current users logged on to the system are*
>
> **who | grep $USER**
>
> **echo** *My current startup directory is*
>
> **pwd**
>
> **echo** *My identification information is*
>
> **id**
>
> **echo** *The processes running on my system are*
>
> **ps**
>
> CTRL-D

Step 3 To save the script and exit to the shell, you should have executed the **:wq** command. To make the script executable, the **chmod +x** *Information* command should have been executed and then the script should have been run by typing *./Information* as shown in Figure 6-1. You should have successfully created and run the script.

Step 4 To redirect the output of the *Information* script to a file named *DailyInfo*, you should have typed the command *./Information* **>** *DailyInfo*. You should have successfully completed the lab and logged off the computer.

```
cathy@localhost:~

File   Edit   Settings   Help

[cathy@localhost cathy]$ vi Information
[cathy@localhost cathy]$ chmod +x Information
[cathy@localhost cathy]$ ./Information
The date today is
Mon Sep  2 01:31:18 CDT 2002
The current users logged on to the system are
cathy     pts/0     Sep  2 01:29 (:0)
My current startup directory is
/home/cathy
My identification information is
uid=500(cathy) gid=500(cathy) groups=500(cathy)
The processes running on my system are
  PID TTY          TIME CMD
 1414 pts/0    00:00:00 bash
 1446 pts/0    00:00:00 bash
 1451 pts/0    00:00:00 ps
[cathy@localhost cathy]$
```

FIGURE 6-1 Output of the *Information* script

Lab Solution 6.02

The following steps should guide you in exploring directories and files:

Step 1   You should have successfully logged on to the Linux computer with your username and password and opened a terminal window.

Step 2   To list the files in your current home directory, you should have typed the **ls** command.

Step 3   To create a new directory called *Novelfiles*, you should have typed **mkdir** *Novelfiles* and confirmed that the new directory exists in your current directory by typing **ls -F | more**. This command lists the objects in the current directory, adding a **/** character to all directory names for identification purposes.

Step 4   You should have moved all files related to Sam's novel to the *Novelfiles* directory by typing **mv** *filename Novelfiles* for each file that you want moved. The files should have included *Chapter_1*, *Chapter_2*, *Chapter_3*, *Chapter_4*, *Novel*, and *Workday* as shown in Figure 6-2.

Step 5   To change your current directory to the *Novelfiles* directory, you should have executed the **cd** *Novelfiles* command and confirmed your location by executing the **pwd** command. You should have executed the **ls** command to verify that you have moved all files successfully and returned to your home directory by executing the **cd** command.

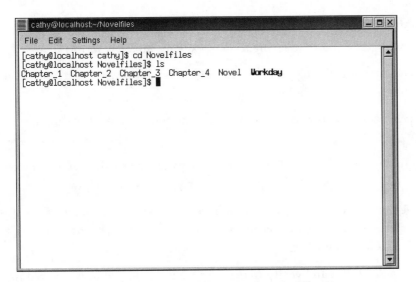

Figure 6-2 List of novel-related files in the *Novelfiles* directory

Step 6   To create a file in the home directory named *Metadata* that lists information about all files listed in the *Novelfiles* directory, you should have typed the command **ls -1** *Novelfiles* | **sort >** *Metadata*. This creates a new file named *Metadata* and sorts the long list of information about all files in the *Novelfiles* directory.

Step 7   To list the contents of the *Novelfiles* directory and confirm that you have created the file successfully, you should have typed the **ls** command. To view the contents of the *Metadata* file, you should have typed **more** *Metadata*. You should have been able to view the file permissions, date modified, and owner for each file. You should have returned to the *Novelfiles* directory with the **cd** *Novelfiles* command.

Step 8   To remove the read permission on the *Chapter_1* file in the new directory, you should have executed the command **chmod -r** *Chapter_1*. You should have returned to the home directory with the **cd** command.

Step 9   To create a new file called *Metadata2* that contains information about all the files in the *Novelfiles* directory, you should have executed the command **ls -1** *Novelfiles* | **sort >** *Metadata2*. Comparing the differences between the *Metadata* and *Metadata2* files can be done by executing the command **comm** *Metadata Metadata2*. The only difference in the two snapshot files should be the permissions change on the *Chapter_1* file that you previously made. You should have successfully completed the lab and logged off the computer.

Lab Solution 6.03

The following steps should guide you in creating a complex word analysis script:

Step 1   You should have successfully logged on to the Linux computer with your username and password and opened a terminal window.

Step 2   You should have added the text content as written to the *Gasoline* file using the visual editor.

Step 3   To create an analysis script called *TestScript* that completes the indicated tasks for the *Gasoline* file, you should have typed the script code exactly as shown in Figure 6-3.

Step 4   To make the *TestScript* executable, you should have executed the command **chmod +x** *TestScript*. To run the script, you should have typed the command *./TestScript*. The results of running the script are shown in Figure 6-4.

Step 5   To open the *ScriptResult* file and verify that the contents match what was asked for in the *TestScript* script, you should have typed **more** *ScriptResult*. You should have successfully completed the lab and logged off the computer.

```
cathy@localhost~

File   Edit   Settings   Help

tr -d '?."!:,();' <  Gasoline \
| tr 'A-Z' 'a-z' \
| tr ' ' '\n' \
| sed '/^$/d' \
| sort | uniq -c \
| sort -rn \
| tee ScriptResult

~
~
~
~
~
~
~
~
~
~
~
~
~
~
~
~
~
"TestScript" 7L, 136C                              7,19        All
```

Figure 6-3 *TestScript* code that is used to analyze the *Gasoline* text file

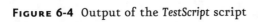

```
cathy@localhost:~                                        _ □ ×
 File   Edit   Settings   Help
[cathy@localhost cathy]$ ./TestScript                    ▲
     5 a
     3 prices
     3 of
     3 gas
     3 gallon
     2 was
     2 the
     2 about
     2 $146
     1 when
     1 weeks
     1 up
     1 unusual
     1 two
     1 trend
     1 to
     1 that
     1 taxes
     1 survey
     1 sunday
     1 steady
     1 stations
     1 since                                             ▼
```

FIGURE 6-4 Output of the *TestScript* script

Chapter 7

Creating and Changing Directories

Lab Exercises

This chapter explores the hierarchical file system and directory structure by navigating through, managing, and creating new directories. Up until now, you have been creating files and saving them in your home directory. On a UNIX/Linux computer, files are stored in different directories depending on the system and user.

You will create directories and subdirectories, and explore the process of changing from one directory to a remote directory or subdirectory. You will also access files within each directory and learn how to efficiently work with file links to directories.

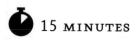 15 MINUTES

Lab Exercise 7.01: Creating Directories

The design firm of Greening Interiors has recently hired Cathy as an interior designer. Cathy wants to create a directory on her Linux computer for hosting all files that pertain to the interior design project she is working on. She has just started the project and wants to save a file called *LivingRoom* in this new directory in order to keep it separate from her other files. She wants to be able to navigate successfully through the file structure of her Linux computer, but also access any information regarding the files in each directory from any directory location.

Learning Objectives

In this lab, you navigate through the file system and create new directories. By the end of this lab, you'll be able to:

- Navigate through the directory structure

- Create a subdirectory

- Change directories

- Create files within a subdirectory

Lab Materials and Setup

The materials you need for this lab are:

- Computer with Red Hat Linux 7.3 installed
- Pencil and paper

Getting Down to Business

The following steps guide you in creating subdirectories. You will have to apply the knowledge that you acquired in the *Introduction to UNIX and Linux* textbook by John Muster (McGraw-Hill/Osborne, 2002) for changing directories and creating files.

Step 1 Log on to the Linux computer with your username and password. Open a terminal window.

Step 2 List the files in your home directory. Create a subdirectory in your home directory called *Design*. List the contents of your home directory to verify that the subdirectory has been created successfully.

Step 3 Change directories to the *Design* subdirectory of your home directory. Confirm your location using the **pwd** command. Create and save a file called *LivingRoom* in the subdirectory with the following contents:

> The look in the living room goes from bland, boring, and cluttered, to pulled-together, smart, and inviting. Shopping finds include all the accessories needed to spruce up the home and the perfect storage solution for the child's toys—baskets, baskets, and more baskets.

Step 4 List the contents of the *Design* subdirectory, including the inode numbers, to ensure that your file has been saved. Return to your home directory.

Step 5 Execute a command to examine the contents of your home directory that distinguishes any directories from files. Obtain a long listing of the *Design* subdirectory contents without navigating to that directory.

Step 6 List the contents of both the current home directory and the *Design* subdirectory. Log off the computer.

 30 MINUTES

Lab Exercise 7.02: Managing Files and Directories

Cathy wants to continue to place all design files in the *Design* subdirectory. She also wants to learn how to manage new files and directories without having to constantly change directories to list or view the files located there. She also wants to create a *Blueprints* subdirectory of the *Design* subdirectory in which to host files that will be sent to her from the architect.

Learning Objectives

In this exercise, you manage files and directories. After you've completed this lab, you will be able to:

- Move files into a subdirectory

- Change filenames when moving files

- Use pathnames to access files and directories

Lab Materials and Setup

The materials you need for this lab are:

- Computer with Red Hat Linux 7.3 installed

- Pencil and paper

- Access to the Internet

Getting Down to Business

The following steps guide you in managing files and directories. You will have to apply the knowledge that you acquired in the *Introduction to UNIX and Linux* textbook by John Muster (McGraw-Hill/Osborne, 2002) for working with pathnames and filenames.

Step 1   Log on to the Linux computer with your username and password. Open a terminal window.

Step 2 From your home directory, create and save the design files shown in the following table:

Filename	Contents
DiningRoom	This room is rather small in size. Measurements need to be taken.
MasterBedroom	This room is extremely large with high ceilings. See architect for additional information.
MasterBathroom	This room will have a new shower added.

Step 3 Move the *DiningRoom* and *MasterBedroom* design files that you just created to the *Design* subdirectory.

Step 4 Without moving from your home directory, verify that the *DiningRoom* and *MasterBedroom* design files are currently listed in your *Design* directory. Attempt to access the *DiningRoom* file. Were you successful? Copy the *MasterBathroom* file from the home directory to the *Design* directory.

_____

_____

Step 5 Move the *MasterBathroom* file to the *Design* directory, but change the file's name to *MBathroom* while doing so. List the contents of the *Design* subdirectory to verify that the file appears with the changed filename.

_____

_____

Step 6 While still in your home directory, execute a command that would remove the copy of the *MasterBathroom* file from the *Design* directory. Note the correct command in the space provided.

_____

_____

Step 7   Change to your *Design* directory and create a subdirectory called *Blueprints*. Change back to your home directory.

Step 8   From your home directory, list the contents of the newly created *Blueprints* directory by indicating the pathname. The *Blueprints* directory should be empty, as it was just created.

Step 9   From your home directory, change to the *Blueprints* directory by executing a command that uses a pathname.

Step 10   From your *Blueprints* directory, execute a command that lists the contents of your home directory. Log off the computer.

 20 MINUTES

Lab Exercise 7.03: Accessing Files in Directories

Cathy wants to learn all available ways to access files in directories, whether she is trying to access a file in a current or remote directory. She understands the use of pathnames to access files, but she also wants to learn any additional methods that are available to her. She also wants to store a file named *LRBlueprint* that she received from an architect in the *Blueprints* subdirectory.

Learning Objectives

In this lab, you access files in several directories using several different methods. After you complete this lab, you will be able to:

- Use parent directory names

- Access files in remote directories

- Return to a previous directory

Lab Materials and Setup

For this lab exercise, you'll need:

- Computer with Red Hat Linux 7.3 installed

- Pencil and paper

Getting Down to Business

The following steps guide you in accessing files in directories. You will have to apply the knowledge that you acquired in the *Introduction to UNIX and Linux* textbook by John Muster (McGraw-Hill/Osborne, 2002) for specifying paths and using parent directory names.

Step 1 Log on to the Linux computer with your username and password. Open a terminal window.

Step 2 From your home directory, change to the *Design* subdirectory. Execute the proper command to obtain a list of the files in the directory. Do dots appear before the filenames in the *Design* directory? Give reasons for your answer.

Step 3 What type of file is the .. (dot dot) file that's indicated in the *Design* directory?

_____

_____

Step 4 Change to the . (dot) directory. Obtain a listing of the files in the directory. What files are displayed?

_____

_____

Step 5 Change to the *Blueprints* directory and create a file called *LRBlueprint*.

Step 6 Change to the *Design* directory. From the *Design* directory, get a listing of the files in your *Blueprints* directory to verify that the *LRBlueprint* file was created successfully.

Step 7 From the *Design* directory, execute a command that you can use to edit the *LRBlueprint* file that you created in the *Blueprints* subdirectory.

Step 8 Change directories to the *Blueprints* directory. Identify the absolute path to your current directory. Log off the computer.

 30 MINUTES

Lab Exercise 7.04: Working with File Links to Directories

Cathy wants to organize the files that exist in her *Design* and *Blueprints* directories so they are easily accessible to her. She has asked for your help in understanding the process of linking files and directories and wants to know if this process will help make her files more easily accessible.

Learning Objectives

In this lab, you work with file links. After you complete this lab, you will be able to:

- Link files to a directory
- Link directories
- Remove linked files and symbolic links
- Rename directories

Lab Materials and Setup

For this lab exercise, you'll need:

- Computer with Red Hat Linux 7.3 installed
- Pencil and paper

Getting Down to Business

The following steps guide you in working with file links to directories. You will have to apply the knowledge that you acquired in the *Introduction to UNIX and Linux* textbook by John Muster (McGraw-Hill/Osborne, 2002) for listing files in directories.

Step 1   Log on to the Linux computer with your username and password. Open a terminal window.

Step 2   From your home directory, change to the *Design* directory. Link the *DiningRoom* file to the *Blueprints* directory with the same filename.

Step 3 Examine the original and linked *DiningRoom* files using the **ls** utility. Can you identify by the output which file is the original and which file is the linked file?

_____

_____

Step 4 Link the *MasterBedroom* and *MBathroom* files to the *Blueprints* directory using the original filenames.

Step 5 Link the *LivingRoom* file to the *Blueprints* directory through the use of a symbolic link. What is the difference between a hard link and a symbolic (soft) link?

_____

_____

Step 6 Link the *Blueprints* directory to the *Design* directory. List the contents of the *Blueprints* directory. How can you identify the symbolic link?

_____

_____

Step 7 Remove the symbolic link from the *LivingRoom* file to the *Blueprints* directory.

Step 8 Attempt to remove the *Blueprints* subdirectory from the *Design* directory by executing the command **rmdir** *Blueprints*. Were you successful? Why or why not?

_____

_____

Step 9 Execute the command that would remove the *Blueprints* directory and all files that exist within the directory. Note the correct command in the space provided.

_____

_____

Step 10 Change the name of the *Design* directory to *DesignBlueprints*. Log off the computer.

Lab Analysis Test

1. What is the result of executing the **pwd** command?

_____

_____

2. How do you explicitly list the files in your home directory without changing directories?

_____

_____

3. How can files be linked to a directory by using a new filename?

_____

_____

4. What issues should be considered when using the **rm -r** command?

_____

_____

5. What is the result of executing the **ls -ld** command?

_____

_____

Key Term Quiz

Use the following vocabulary terms to complete the sentences below. Not all of the terms will be used.

cd *pathname*

ln

ln -s

ls -a

ls -F

ls -i

ls -ld

mkdir

rmdir

rm -r

1. The _____ command displays a list of files and subdirectories in your current directory, including files with names beginning with a period/dot.

2. The _____ command lists filenames and their associated inodes in the current directory.

3. The _____ command displays the names of files in your current directory and places a slash after directory names. Executable files are displayed with an *.

4. The _____ command removes a directory, but only if it does not contain files or subdirectories.

5. The _____ command is used to create a symbolic link.

Lab Wrap-Up

In this chapter, you navigated through the file system, created directories, copied and moved files into directories, and accessed files using pathnames. You listed files in multiple directories and removed directories in the file system. You also worked with hard and soft links to directories and changed the name of a directory. You should now be comfortable with navigating through the directory structure, as well as creating and accessing files and directories.

Solutions

In this section, you'll find solutions to the Lab Exercises.

Lab Solution 7.01

The following steps should guide you in creating directories:

Step 1   You should have successfully logged on to the Linux computer with your username and password and opened a terminal window.

Step 2   To list the files in your home directory, you should have executed the **ls | more** command or simply the **ls** command. To create a subdirectory in your home directory called *Design*, you should have executed the command **mkdir** *Design*. Listing the contents of your home directory to verify that the subdirectory has been created successfully can be done using the **ls | more** command.

Step 3   To change directories to the *Design* subdirectory, you should have executed the **cd** *Design* command. Confirming your location using the **pwd** command displays an output of your current location on the screen. To create and save a file called *LivingRoom* in the subdirectory with the indicated contents shown in Figure 7-1, you should have opened the **vi** editor by typing **vi** *LivingRoom* and typed the contents. You should have then saved the file by executing the **:wq** command.

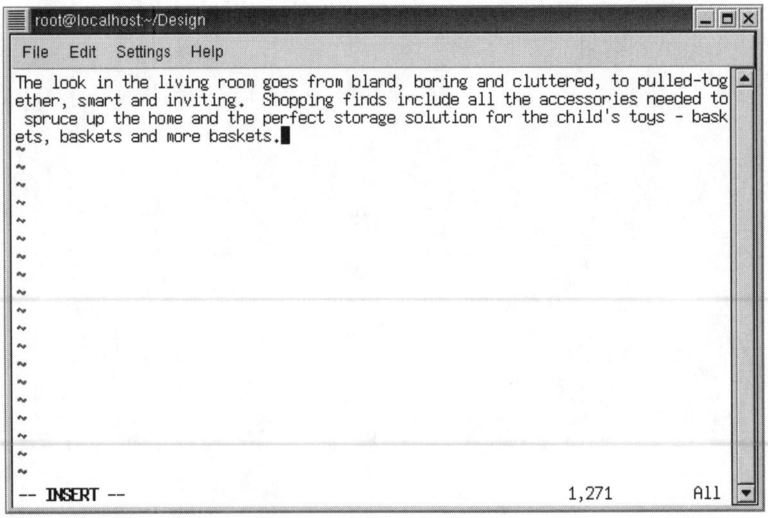

FIGURE 7-1 *LivingRoom* file contents

Step 4 To list the contents of the *Design* subdirectory, including the inode numbers, you should have executed the **list** command with the **-I** option, or **ls -i**. Returning to your home directory could have been accomplished by typing the **cd** command.

Step 5 Examining the contents of your home directory and distinguishing all directories from files is done by executing the command **ls -F | more**. The **-F** option adds a slash to the end of any directory. To obtain a long listing of the *Design* subdirectory contents without navigating to that directory, you should have executed the command **ls -l** *Design*. This will not change directories, only show a long list of the files located in the subdirectory.

Step 6 To list the contents of both the current home directory and the *Design* subdirectory, you should have typed the command **ls -R -C | more**. You should have successfully completed the lab and logged off the computer.

Lab Solution 7.02

The following steps should guide you in managing files in directories:

Step 1 You should have successfully logged on to the Linux computer with your username and password and opened a terminal window.

Step 2 From your home directory, you should have created and saved the *DiningRoom*, *MasterBedroom*, and *MasterBathroom* design files using the **vi** editor with the indicated contents shown in Figures 7-2, 7-3, and 7-4.

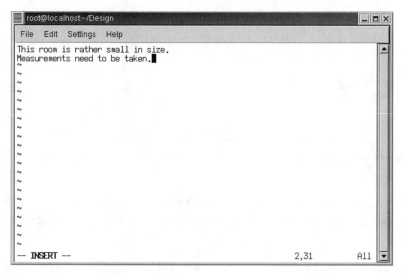

Figure 7-2 *DiningRoom* file contents

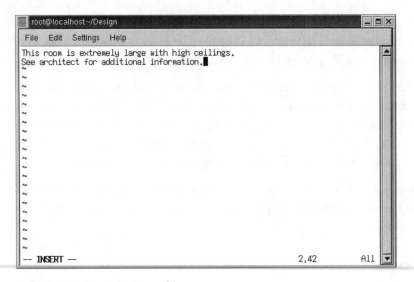

FIGURE 7-3 *MasterBedroom* file contents

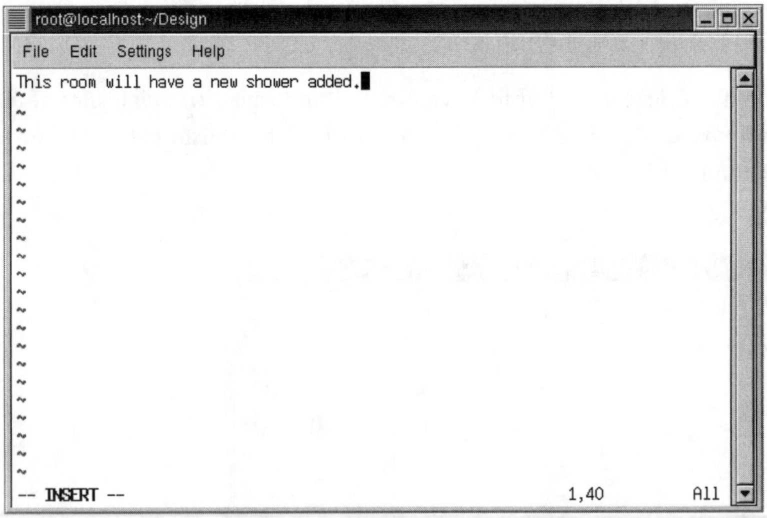

FIGURE 7-4 *MasterBathroom* file contents

Step 3 To move the *DiningRoom* and *MasterBedroom* design files that you just created to the *Design* subdirectory, you should have executed the command **mv** *DiningRoom MasterBedroom Design.*

Step 4 Without moving from your home directory, you should have verified that the *DiningRoom* and *MasterBedroom* design files were listed in the *Design* directory by executing the command **ls** *Design*. You should have been successful in your attempt to access the *DiningRoom* file by executing the command **more** *Design/DiningRoom*. To copy the *MasterBathroom* file from the home directory to the *Design* directory, you should have executed the command **cp** *Master-Bathroom Design/*.

Step 5 Moving the *MasterBathroom* file to the *Design* directory and changing the file's name to *MBathroom* while doing so can be done by executing the command **mv** *MasterBathroom Design/MBathroom*. To verify that the file appears with the changed filename in the *Design* subdirectory, you should have executed the command **ls** *Design*.

Step 6 From your home directory, you should have executed the command **rm** *Design/MasterBathroom* to remove the copy of the *MasterBathroom* file from the *Design* directory, and confirmed the removal by entering *yes* at the prompt.

Step 7 To change to your *Design* directory and create a subdirectory called *Blueprints*, you should have executed the commands **cd** *Design* and **mkdir** *Blueprints*. To change back to your home directory, you should have executed the command **cd**.

Step 8 From your home directory, you should have listed the contents of the newly created *Blueprints* directory by executing the pathname **ls** *Design/Blueprints*. The *Blueprints* directory should be empty, as it was just created.

Step 9 From your home directory, you should have changed to the *Blueprints* directory by executing the command **cd** *Design/Blueprints*.

Step 10 From your *Blueprints* directory, you should have executed the command **ls** ~ to list the contents of your home directory. You should have successfully completed the lab and logged off the computer.

Lab Solution 7.03

The following steps should guide you in accessing files in directories:

Step 1 You should have successfully logged on to the Linux computer with your username and password and opened a terminal window.

Step 2 To change to the *Design* subdirectory from your home directory, you should have executed the command **cd** *Design*. After executing the **ls -a** command to obtain a list of the files in the directory, you should have obtained the results shown in Figure 7-5. Dots should have appeared before the filenames in the *Design* directory. The single dot indicates the local directory, whereas the double dots indicate the home directory.

Step 3 The .. file that's indicated in the *Design* directory is a directory file.

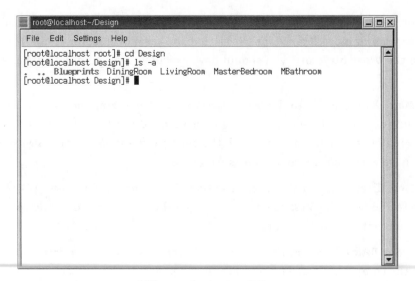

```
root@localhost~/Design                                    _ □ X
File  Edit  Settings  Help
[root@localhost root]# cd Design
[root@localhost Design]# ls -a
.  ..  Blueprints  DiningRoom  LivingRoom  MasterBedroom  MBathroom
[root@localhost Design]# █
```

FIGURE 7-5 Listing of files in the *Design* directory

Step 4　You should have executed the command **cd ..** to change to the .. (dot) directory, To obtain a listing of the files in the directory, you should have executed the command **ls**. All files and directories in the home directory are displayed.

Step 5　To change to the *Blueprints* directory, you should have executed the command **cd** *Design/Blueprints*. To create a file called *LRBlueprint* in that directory, you should have executed the command **vi** *LRBlueprint*.

Step 7　You should have executed the command **cd ..** to change to the *Design* directory. To get a listing of the files in your *Blueprints* directory, you should have executed the command **ls** *Design/Blueprints*.

Step 8　From the *Design* directory, you should have executed the **vi** *~/Blueprints/LRBlueprint* command to edit the *LRBlueprint* file that you created in the *Blueprints* subdirectory.

Step 9　To change to the *Blueprints* directory, you should have executed the command **cd** *Blueprints*. You should have executed the **pwd** command to identify the absolute path to your current directory. You should have successfully completed the lab and logged off the computer.

Lab Solution 7.04

The following steps should guide you in working with file links:

Step 1　You should have successfully logged on to the Linux computer with your username and password and opened a terminal window.

Step 2   To change to the *Design* directory from your home directory, you should have executed the command **cd** *Design*. To link the *DiningRoom* file to the *Blueprints* directory with the same filename, you should have executed the command **ln** *DiningRoom Blueprints*.

Step 3   The original and linked *DiningRoom* files can be compared using the **ls -li** utility for each directory. You should not be able to identify by the output which file is the original and which file is the linked file. They should appear to be associated with the same inode number.

Step 4   To link the *MasterBedroom* and *MBathroom* files to the *Blueprints* directory using the original filenames, you should have executed the command **ln** *MasterBedroom MBathroom Blueprints*.

Step 5   To link the *LivingRoom* file to the *Blueprints* directory through the use of a symbolic link, you should have changed to the *Blueprints* directory by executing the command **cd** *Blueprints* and then executed the command **ln -s ~/***LivingRoom*. The difference between a hard link and a symbolic (soft) link is that a symbolic link is a small file in the current directory that contains the information needed to locate the linked file wherever it is actually listed. A hard link is a listing of a file in a directory.

Step 6   To link the *Blueprints* directory to the *Design* directory, you should have executed the command **ln -s ~/***Design*. To list the contents of the *Blueprints* directory, you should have executed the command **cd** *Design* to change to the *Design* directory and then executed the command **ls -F** *Blueprints*. This command shows the @ symbol following the linked *Design* directory, indicating that it is a symbolic link. The result is shown in Figure 7-6.

Step 7   To remove the symbolic link from the *LivingRoom* file to the *Blueprints* directory, you should have changed to the *Blueprints* directory by executing the command **cd** *Blueprints* and then executed the command **rm** *LivingRoom*.

Step 8   You attempted to remove the *Blueprints* subdirectory from the *Design* directory by executing the command **cd ..** to change to the *Design* directory and then executing the command **rmdir** *Blueprints*. This command should have failed because the *Blueprints* directory was not empty. You should have received an error message stating this.

Step 9   You should have executed the command **rm -r** *Blueprints* in order to remove the *Blueprints* directory and all files that exist within the directory.

Step 10   To change the name of the *Design* directory to *DesignBlueprints*, you should have changed to the home directory by executing the command **cd** and then executed the command **mv** *Design DesignBlueprints*. You should have successfully completed the lab and logged off the computer.

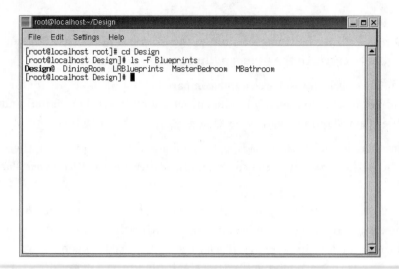

FIGURE 7-6 Symbolic link to the *Design* directory

Chapter 8

Specifying Instructions to the Shell

Lab Exercises

In previous chapters, you entered several commands. In this chapter, you will expand your knowledge of the command line. You will use wildcards and command substitution to create powerful commands. You will also redirect the errors from your commands to a log file. Each of these skills is very useful in both academic and corporate settings.

 15 MINUTES

Lab Exercise 8.01: Identifying Portions of the Command Line

Your friend LaTrina is about to graduate from college. At her school, she had access to a UNIX system. She created and published a fantastic web page and service called Go4U. Go4U is a system that delivers anything to anybody. The registered user simply has to list what they would like delivered and where. Go4U's delivery people will pick up the package and deliver it on time.

Since LaTrina is graduating, she is losing her web space. She has registered her new domain and would like help moving the web page to her hosting company. Her hosting company is using a different variant of UNIX than her college. LaTrina, while being an excellent web developer, only learned enough UNIX to publish her page. She is anticipating some problems with the conversion and has asked your help with the move. You, being the UNIX expert, have agreed to teach her some basics and fix any UNIX bugs.

Before you teach LaTrina any advanced commands, you want to ensure that she understands how a UNIX command is built. You will have her dissect and build several complex UNIX commands. This will allow her to understand the commands she enters later.

Learning Objectives

In this lab, you will identify portions of a command line. After you've completed this lab, you will be able to:

- Identify utilities, parameters, and switches
- Build UNIX commands

Lab Materials and Setup

The materials you need for this lab are:

- Pencil and paper

Getting Down to Business

The following steps will help you identify the different portions of a command line. You will have to apply the knowledge that you acquired in the *Introduction to UNIX and Linux* textbook by John Muster (McGraw-Hill/Osborne, 2002) for working with the command line.

Step 1   Identify the utilities, switches, and parameters in the following commands. For each command line in the following list, write the utilities, parameters, and switches present.

Command Line	Utilities	Parameters	Switches
ls	_____	_____	_____
cp /etc/printcap .;less printcap	_____	_____	_____
man ls -d	_____	_____	_____
mkdir -m755 scripts;cd scripts	_____	_____	_____

Step 2   In the space provided, fill in the portion of the command line that could be present.

a) _____

b) _____ _____ _____

c) _____; _____ _____

Step 3   For each of the above command lines, create three valid commands that would fill each space. As an example, for b, a valid command is **cp /etc/printcap ~/printcap**.

a) _____

b) _____

c) _____

 10 MINUTES

Lab Exercise 8.02: Finding Utilities on the System

Much of LaTrina's site was built using the Perl programming language. Perl is a very nice language for web developers. It is easy to learn and reasonably fast. It is also freely available for download at several web sites. For a Perl script to run, the script must know what directory holds the working version of Perl.

LaTrina's site currently does not work because she has the wrong path to Perl. In order for the Perl scripts to run, the first line must contain the actual path to the **perl** command. LaTrina's script is still set to the Perl directory at her university. The line incorrectly reads **#!/usr/sbin/perl**. She asks you to help her find the correct location.

Learning Objectives

In this exercise, you will find several commands on the system. After you've completed this lab, you will be able to:

- Use **whereis** to find all occurrences of a utility
- Use **find** to find the directory holding a utility
- Use **which** to determine which of the occurrences is currently the system default

Lab Materials and Setup

The materials you need for this lab are:

- Computer with Red Hat Linux 7.3 installed
- Pencil and paper

Getting Down to Business

✔ Hint

Three utilities can help in this situation. The **whereis** utility will find all versions of the utility. The **find** utility will give you the directory, but not the path holding the current default version. The **which** utility will determine the current default version.

The following steps will help you locate commands on the system. You will use three different tools to find several commands. You will have to apply the knowledge that you acquired in the *Introduction to UNIX and Linux* textbook by John Muster (McGraw-Hill/Osborne, 2002) for searching the UNIX/Linux installation.

Locate the following utilities using **find**, **whereis**, and **which**. Record the results in the table. Feel free to abbreviate if the results are very long.

Utility	find	whereis	which
perl	_____	_____	_____
ls	_____	_____	_____
man	_____	_____	_____
startx	_____	_____	_____

 20 MINUTES

Lab Exercise 8.03: Using Command Substitution to Write Simple Scripts

LaTrina's hosting provider does not allow her to write simple shell scripts. This is a problem as she is used to scripting. One task that will be particularly onerous will be her daily counts. She prides her organization on having a 1-hour turnaround on deliveries. She checks this by counting the number of requests and the number of deliveries. The numbers should be the same or very close. LaTrina's web page writes the requests and deliveries to files called *requests.txt* and *deliveries.txt*, respectively. In addition, she has several other files for which she needs a daily count.

LaTrina would like you to give her one command that will count the *requests.txt*, *deliveries.txt*, *errors.txt*, *users.txt*, and *links.txt* files. You would like to use a shell script, but the UNIX shell will not allow it. You decide to use the command substitution features of UNIX.

Learning Objectives

In this lab, you will simulate the directory structure of LaTrina's web site on your account. By the end of this lab, you'll be able to:

- Create a text file using a text editor

- Use command substitution to automate a process

Lab Materials and Setup

The materials you need for this lab are:

- Computer with Red Hat Linux 7.3 installed

- Access to **pico**, **vi**, or another text editor

Getting Down to Business

In the following steps you will practice using the command substitution features of UNIX. You will have to apply the knowledge that you acquired in the *Introduction to UNIX and Linux* textbook by John Muster (McGraw-Hill/Osborne, 2002) for working with command substitution.

Step 1   Create five text files filled with random lines of text. Name these files *requests.txt*, *deliveries.txt*, *errors.txt*, *users.txt*, and *links.txt*.

Step 2   Create a text file with the names of the fives text files, one name on each line.

Step 3   Using the ` `` ` syntax, create a command that counts each of the text files.

Step 4   Run your command. Verify that it correctly counts the files.

 15 MINUTES

Lab Exercise 8.04: Writing Wildcard Expressions

There are several hundred files on LaTrina's web site. Periodically, she needs to modify entire groups of files. For example, she often updates the *.htm* files. Before updating the files, she copies the files into a backup directory. She currently does this one file at a time and would like a faster method. Wildcards will allow her to access and manipulate large numbers of files at one time.

Learning Objectives

In this lab, you will write wildcard expressions. By the end of this lab, you'll be able to:

- Use the * (asterisk) operator to write expressions
- Use the ? (question mark) operator to write expressions
- Use the [ ] (brackets) operator to write expressions

Lab Materials and Setup

The materials you need for this lab are:

- Pencil and paper
- (Optional) Computer with Red Hat Linux 7.3 installed

Getting Down to Business

You will practice writing wildcard expressions in the following tables. In the first table, you will describe the command and list possible results. In the second table, you will create commands to solve the problem. In each case, an example is provided for guidance. You will have to apply the knowledge that you acquired in the *Introduction to UNIX and Linux* textbook by John Muster (McGraw-Hill/Osborne, 2002) for working with wildcards.

Command	Description of Wildcard	Example Files
ls *a**	All files that begin with *a*	*apple, Andrew, a.out*
ls *duke**.doc	_____	_____
ls **.jpg*	_____	_____

Command	Description of Wildcard	Example Files
ls ???.jpg	_____	_____
ls a?.jpg	_____	_____
ls m[aeiou]d	_____	_____
ls [d-g]o[gt]	_____	_____

Write a wildcard expression that will address the requirement.

Requirement	Wildcard
All files that begin with _ga_	_ga_*
All files that begin with _g_ and end with _.doc_	_____
All files that begin with any vowel and have exactly two letters after the vowel	_____
All files that are three letters long, the last of which is a letter between _g_ and _k_	_____

 25 MINUTES

Lab Exercise 8.05: Redirecting Errors

LaTrina is a very talented programmer. Her web site currently responds to user or site errors by writing to a web log. This is the default action on a web site. LaTrina wishes to handle her own errors. She understands the programming code involved, but does not understand the UNIX aspect. She asks you to help.

She has a program called **regist.exe** that will run on her web site. **regist** allows her customers to create an account. **regist** works pretty well, but there is the occasional bug. LaTrina would like the error messages redirected into the *errors.txt* file.

Learning Objectives

In this lab, you will redirect error messages from commands to a file. By the end of this lab, you'll be able to:

- Redirect error messages from programs to a user-defined log

- Run programs in the background

Lab Materials and Setup

The materials you need for this lab are:

- Computer with Red Hat Linux 7.3 installed

- (Optional) A program called **regist.exe**

Getting Down to Business

The following steps will help you master redirecting error output into a file. You will need a working program that writes error output. You will have to apply the knowledge that you acquired in the *Introduction to UNIX and Linux* textbook by John Muster (McGraw-Hill/Osborne, 2002) for redirecting errors.

✔ **Hint**

UNIX allows you to redirect the errors from a program into a text file. The redirection operator is **2>** or **2>>**. The **2** indicates that this is error redirection. **>** and **>>** act as in earlier chapters; the **>** overwrites the file and **>>** appends to the file.

OPTIONAL

If you want to verify that the redirection works, a simple program is needed. Using **pico** or **vi**, create the following C++ program named **regist.cpp**:

```
#include <iostream.h>

void main()

{

    cout << "This is on the screen\n";

    cerr << "This is in the error log\n";

}
```

You will need to compile the program before it can run. The command to compile is **g++ regist.cpp -oregist.exe**. If no messages appear, you can run the program by typing **regist.exe**. If any errors occur, verify that you have typed and named the program correctly.

✔ **Hint**

A compiled version of **regist.exe** can be found at **www.Osborne.com**. Enter the ISBN for this text and click on the **Downloads For This Book** link.

Step 1   Write or acquire the program. If **regist.exe** is unavailable, you can substitute *bash*. To test, enter bad commands like **1k** or **wc -z**.

Step 2   Using the **2>>** and **&** operators, write the command that will run **regist.exe** in the background, redirecting errors to the error log.

Step 3   Run your command three times. If you did everything right, your error message should be in the file three times.

 10 MINUTES

Lab Exercise 8.06: Gathering Error Numbers

With redirection error, LaTrina can now implement all of the error checks, and check her own log file for messages. This will allow her to customize the program to trap every error the user generates. In time, her **regist.exe** will be crash-proof.

She asks you how she can get the error codes for common UNIX errors. She knows what errors she is getting, but without the error codes she cannot program for the errors. You tell her about the **$?** variable, which holds the error code for the previous error.

Learning Objectives

In this lab, you will record error numbers for common commands. By the end of this lab, you'll be able to:

- Determine the error code for any UNIX error

Lab Materials and Setup

The materials you need for this lab are:

- Computer with Red Hat Linux 7.3 installed
- Pencil and paper

Getting Down to Business

The following table has several commands. Run the command and get the error number using the **$?** variable. Record the error number in the space provided. Recall that you will need to echo this variable to get the contents. You will have to apply the knowledge that you acquired in the *Introduction to UNIX and Linux* textbook by John Muster (McGraw-Hill/Osborne, 2002) for echoing variable contents.

✖ Warning

Do not log in as root to run this exercise!

Command	Error Code
ls	_____
ls -e	_____
sleep(8)	_____
ls >> /etc/termcap	_____
gg	_____

 30 MINUTES

Lab Exercise 8.07: Modifying the *bash* Environment

LaTrina will be spending a lot of time on her new site. You decide to modify her environment to make her work easier. You know that you can create aliases for common commands, set the *noclobber* variable, and set the variables used in her scripts to be available to all child processes. These modifications are done to the *.bash_profile* file.

You will modify LaTrina's *.bash_profile* file. This file controls the environment for **bash** users. **bash** is a very common shell on UNIX systems. You will set the *noclobber* variable, create some new variables that LaTrina uses in her scripts, create aliases to "safer" UNIX commands, and modify her path statement to include a new directory. Using the *noclobber* variable and setting the interactive mode on the utilities **mv**, **cp**, and **rm** can protect the files. You will make the shell easier to use by setting a path to her *commands* directory and an alias for the command you created in Lab Exercise 8.03.

> ✖ **Warning**
>
> Be sure you have approval before modifying your *.bash_profile*. At some schools, this offense can lead to expulsion.

Learning Objectives

In this lab, you will modify your UNIX profile. By the end of this lab, you'll be able to:

- Set the *noclobber* variable
- Create and export variables
- Create aliases
- Modify a path

Lab Materials and Setup

The materials you need for this lab are:

- Computer with Red Hat Linux 7.3 installed

- Permission from the lab administrator to modify your profile

Getting Down to Business

The following steps will allow you to modify the *.bash_profile* file on a UNIX/Linux computer. You will have to apply the knowledge that you acquired in the *Introduction to UNIX and Linux* textbook by John Muster (McGraw-Hill/Osborne, 2002) for creating aliases.

✖ Warning

Be sure to back up your original version of *.bash_profile*. This will allow you to recover from any serious errors you make.

Step 1   Create a directory called *commands*.

Step 2   Make a backup copy of your *.bash_profile* file. This file is found in your home directory. Copy it to the same directory as *orig_profile*.

Step 3   Using a text editor, edit your *.bash_profile* to include the following:

- An alias for **cp** to **cp -i**

- An alias for **mv** to **mv -i**

- An alias for **rm** to **rm -i**

- An alias called **countem** that points to the command you created in Lab Exercise 8.03

- Add the *commands* directory to the path

- Create and export a variable called *SITE* that holds the web address **www.go4u.com**

- Set *noclobber* on

Step 4   Log off and log back in. Verify that there are no errors. Check your aliases, variables, and path statements. Run the **countem** alias.

If desired, you can replace the *.bash_profile* with the *orig_profile*. No harm will come if you leave the changes in your file.

Lab Analysis Test

1. How many different words can be composed with the following wildcards? [*agtz*][*enk*][*alp*]

_____

_____

2. Why is it important to create a backup of the *.bash_profile* file before modifying it?

_____

_____

3. What is the primary difference between **which** and **whereis**?

_____

_____

4. What does the *noclobber* variable prevent?

_____

_____

5. What is the result of the following command? `ls /usr/games/f*`

_____

_____

Key Term Quiz

Use the following vocabulary terms to complete the sentences below. Not all of the terms will be used.

$?	find
*	noclobber
.bash_profile	parameters
?	PATH
[]	redirection
2>	set
2>>	switches
alias	tokens
command substitution	whereis
error number	which
export	

1. To turn on the *noclobber* variable, you use the command _____ **-o noclobber**.

2. The _____ command returns the child directory, but not the entire file for a command.

3. The **$?** variable generates the _____ of the previous command.

4. In the command **ls /etc**, the **/etc** is a _____.

5. After filling a variable with a value, you must _____ it so it is available to child processes.

6. The _____ variable provides the directories that UNIX will search for a command.

7. The pieces of a command line are referred to as _____.

8. The _____ wildcard will match any number of characters.

9. In UNIX, _____ are preceded with a -.

10. To use _____ on a UNIX command, you enclose the desired command in ` `.

Lab Wrap-Up

You have modified a web site environment to simplify the owner's UNIX experience. You also redirected the output from the **regist.exe** program to a custom log. You generated an alias that used the command substitution feature of UNIX to create a command called **countem** that counts the site's logs. Finally, you practiced working with wildcards and generating errors. Understanding how the command line works allows you to learn new, complex commands more easily.

Solutions

In this section, you'll find solutions to the Lab Exercises.

Lab Solution 8.01

The following steps allow you to identify the different portions of a command line:

Step 1

Command Line	Utilities	Parameters	Switches
ls	ls		
cp /etc/printcap .;less printcap	cp, less	/etc/printcap, printcap	
man ls -d	man	ls	-d
mkdir -m755 scripts;cd scripts	mkdir, cd	755, scripts	-m

Step 2

    a)   utility

    b)   utility switch or parameter switch or parameter

    c)   utility; utility switch or parameter

Step 3

    a)   ls, pwd, cal

    b)   ls -l /etc, man -D man, mv first second

    c)   who;date -u, ls; ls *.cpp, pwd;cd ..

Lab Solution 8.02

The following table provides the correct command for each search. Each of the utilities (**find**, **whereis**, and **which**) require one parameter: the utility to find. Thus, **which perl** will find the current version of Perl on your system. See the following table for the appropriate commands:

Utility	find	whereis	which
perl	find perl	whereis perl	which perl
ls	find ls	whereis ls	which ls

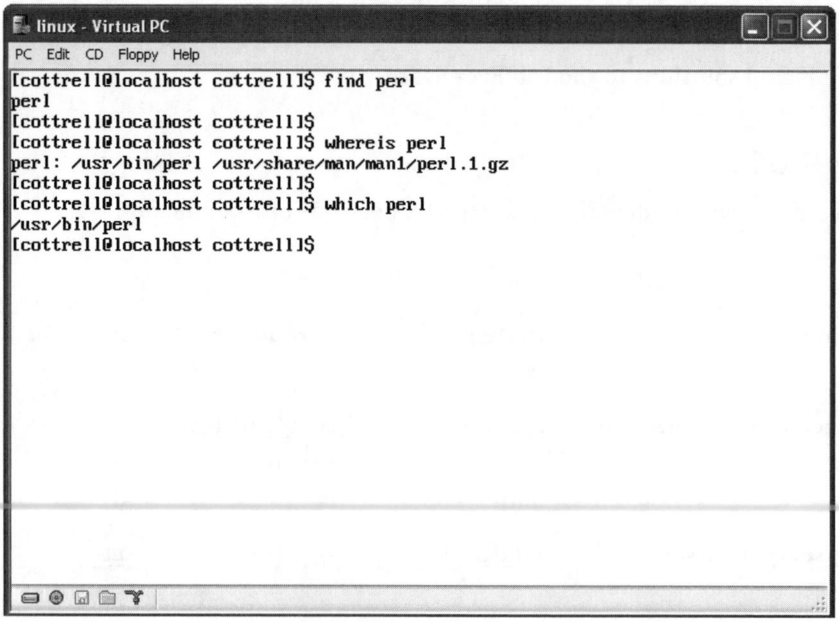

```
 linux - Virtual PC                                          _ □ X
PC  Edit  CD  Floppy  Help
[cottrell@localhost cottrell]$ find perl
perl
[cottrell@localhost cottrell]$
[cottrell@localhost cottrell]$ whereis perl
perl: /usr/bin/perl /usr/share/man/man1/perl.1.gz
[cottrell@localhost cottrell]$
[cottrell@localhost cottrell]$ which perl
/usr/bin/perl
[cottrell@localhost cottrell]$




```

FIGURE 8-1 Results of the **perl** searches

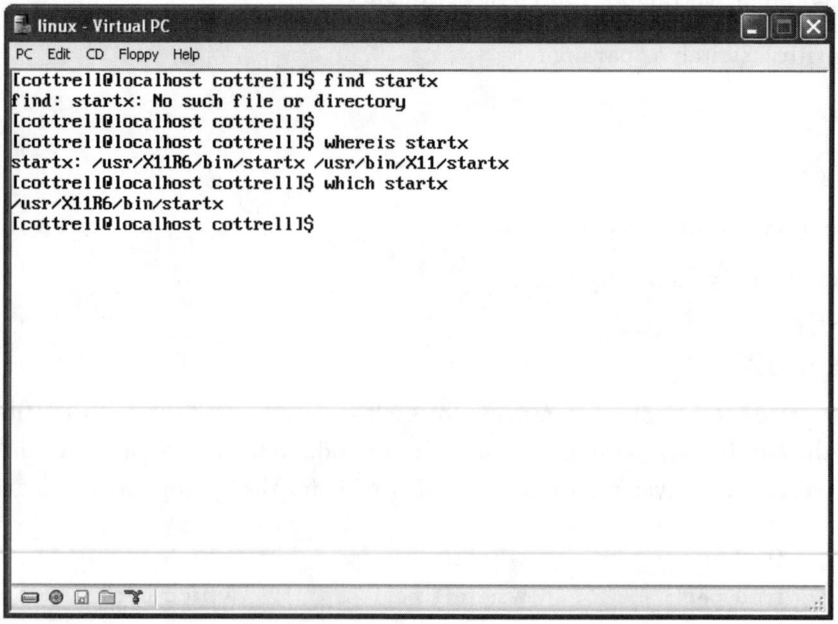

```
 linux - Virtual PC                                          _ □ X
PC  Edit  CD  Floppy  Help
[cottrell@localhost cottrell]$ find startx
find: startx: No such file or directory
[cottrell@localhost cottrell]$
[cottrell@localhost cottrell]$ whereis startx
startx: /usr/X11R6/bin/startx /usr/bin/X11/startx
[cottrell@localhost cottrell]$ which startx
/usr/X11R6/bin/startx
[cottrell@localhost cottrell]$




```

FIGURE 8-2 Results of the **startx** searches

Utility	find	whereis	which
man	find man	whereis man	which man
startx	find startx	whereis startx	which startx

Figure 8-1 shows the results of the **perl** searches and Figure 8-2 shows the **startx** search results.

Lab Solution 8.03

The following steps should guide you in using the command substitution features of UNIX:

Step 1   You should have created the five text files using **pico** or your favorite text editor. Then you should have typed several lines in each, and written down the length of each file.

_____

_____

Step 2   Again using **pico**, you should have created a file called *logs* that contained the names *requests.txt*, *deliveries.txt*, *errors.txt*, *users.txt*, and *links.txt*. Each should have been placed on their own line. The following listing provides an example of the *logs* file:

```
requests.txt
deliveries.txt
errors.txt
users.txt
links.txt
```

Step 3   Using **wc**, the **-l** switch, and the **cat** command, you should have counted each file. The following listing provides the command for the **bash** shell:

wc -l `cat logs`

Figure 8-3 provides the output for a sample run of the command.

```
linux - Virtual PC                                    _ □ X
PC   Edit   CD   Floppy   Help
[cottrell@localhost chapter9]$ wc -l `cat logs`
     10 requests.txt
     10 deliveries.txt
      1 errors.txt
     60 users.txt
     20 links.txt
    101 total
[cottrell@localhost chapter9]$
```

FIGURE 8-3 Sample output of the command

Lab Solution 8.04

In this lab, you worked with three of the wildcards in UNIX. The character * can replace any character or any number of characters. For example, **a*** lists files like *a*, *ab*, *abc*, *abcd*, and so on. The **?** matches any one character. For example, **???** will find any three-letter filename. It will not find filenames with two or four characters; only three characters are returned. The **[]** denotes either a list of characters that can be used or a range of characters. **[a-f]** is all letters from *a* through *f* inclusive. **[aeiou]** includes the letters *aeiou* only.

Command	Description of Wildcard	Example Files
ls *a**	All files that begin with *a*	*apple, Andrew, a.out*
ls *duke**.doc*	All files that begin with duke and end with .doc	*dukeCity.doc, dukeWayne.doc, duke.doc*
ls *.jpg*	All files that end with .jpg	*lee.jpg, lizzie.jpg, Christopher.jpg*
ls ???.jpg*	All three-letter files that end with .jpg	*lee.jpg, dad.jpg, mom.jpg*

Command	Description of Wildcard	Example Files
ls *a?.jpg*	All two-letter .jpg files starting with *a*	*al.jpg, am.jpg*
ls m[aeiou]d	Three-letter words starting with *m* followed by a vowel, ending in *d*	*mad, med, mid, mod, mud*
ls [d-g]o[gt]	Three-letter words, starting with *d, e, f, g* having *o* as the middle letter, ending with *g* or *t*	*dog, dot, eog, eot, fog, fot, gog, got*

Requirement	Wildcard
All files that begin with *ga*	*ga**
All files that begin with *g* and end with *.doc*	*g*.doc*
All files that begin with any vowel and have exactly two letters after the vowel	*[aeiou]??*
All files that are three letters long, the last of which is a letter between *g* and *k*	*??[g-k]*

Lab Solution 8.05

The following steps will allow you to redirect the error output to a file:

Step 1 You should have written the program with **pico**, making sure to type the lines correctly, including the proper punctuation. You should have then compiled with **g++ regist.cpp -oregist.exe**.

Step 2 You should have executed the command **regist.exe 2>>** *errors.txt* **&..**

Step 3 You should have executed the command two more times and then run **cat** *errors.txt*. You should have seen the message three times in the file.

Lab Solution 8.06

The following table provides the error codes for several common errors. The command to get an error code is **echo $?**. This must be executed immediately after the error message.

Command	Error Code
ls	0
ls -e	1
sleep(8)	258
ls >> /etc/termcap	1
gg	127

Lab Solution 8.07

The following steps will modify your *.bash_profile* file.

Step 1   You should have changed to your home directory using **cd ~**. You should then have created the *commands* directory with **mkdir** *commands*.

Step 2   You should have made a backup copy of the *.bash_profile* file with **cp** *.bash_profile orig_profile*.

Step 3   You should have edited your profile with your favorite text editor. Then you should have added the following lines to the end of your script:

SITE=*www.go4u.com*

set -o noclobber

alias countem='wc -l `cat logs`'

alias cp='cp -i'

alias rm='rm -i'

alias mv='mv -i'

PATH=$PATH:$HOME/commands

export PATH SITE

Step 4   You should have tested your changes by running the commands **alias** and **env**. Your aliases and new variables should be listed. You should then have tested your **countem** alias. It should have worked as before.

Chapter 9

Setting File and Directory Permissions

Lab Exercises

You have mastered working with the command line and entering commands. Along the way you learned how to write simple shell scripts. In this chapter, you will learn how to set permissions on a file and directory. You will write a script that archives a series of files and will set a global permission mask, called an **umask**.

 15 MINUTES

Lab Exercise 9.01: Defining Permissions Based on Number

LaTrina has a problem. Some of her web services and pages are not running. She is getting permissions errors in Internet Explorer. She does not know why these programs will not run; they ran at her old site. In addition to this problem, she needs a way to archive data on her site. You immediately suspect she has a permissions problem. You agree to help her and teach her some basic UNIX permissions along the way.

The command to fix most of LaTrina's problem is **chmod**, which changes the mode (file permissions) on a file. True UNIX users use the numeric parameters for **chmod** rather than the letter equivalents. In this exercise, you will practice reading and setting permissions.

Learning Objectives

In this lab, you will identify permissions on files. By the end of this lab, you'll be able to:

- Convert numeric permissions to letter permissions
- Create numeric permissions based on need

Lab Materials and Setup

The materials you need for this lab are:

- Pencil and paper

Getting Down to Business

The following lab asks you to describe the permissions on a series of files. You will have to apply the knowledge that you acquired in the *Introduction to UNIX and Linux* textbook by John Muster (McGraw-Hill/Osborne, 2002) for working with numeric permissions.

Step 1   Based on the numbers presented below, describe and enter the permissions for the owner, group, and other users in the following list.

Permission	Owner	Group	Other
777	read, write, execute	read, write, execute	read, write, execute
644	_____	_____	_____
640	_____	_____	_____
751	_____	_____	_____
711	_____	_____	_____
700	_____	_____	_____

Step 2   Based on the needs described below, create and enter the permission number in the following list.

Need	Numeric Equivalent
Owner can read and write, group can read and write, other cannot do anything	_____
Owner can read, write, and execute; group and other can execute	_____
Owner can read and write, group can read, other can read and write	_____
Owner can read and write, group and other can read	_____

 25 MINUTES

Lab Exercise 9.02: Creating an Archive Script

The Go4U web site maintained by LaTrina generates a lot of text files. These files are very important to the continued maintenance of the site. Periodically, LaTrina makes a copy of the files into a separate directory. Currently she handles this manually, but would like to have a script to make this easier. She has obtained permission from her hosting company to author and run shell scripts on her site.

You will write a script that copies all of the *.txt*, *.dat*, *.html*, and *.cgi* files from their directories to the *archive* directory. By placing the script in the *command* directory, LaTrina can run the script from anywhere on her site.

Learning Objectives

In this lab, you will write an archive script. By the end of this lab, you'll be able to:

- Write a script
- Make the script executable

Lab Materials and Setup

The materials you need for this lab are:

- Computer with Red Hat Linux 7.3 installed
- The *command* directory in your PATH

✔ Hint

You may need to create several files and folders. You can use the **touch** command to create files. The syntax is **touch** *filename*, where *filename* is the name of the file you are going to create. Several files can be created at one time. Thus, you can create several blank *.txt*, *.dat*, *.html*, and *.cgi* files for practice.

Getting Down to Business

The following steps will help you create a script called *archive* that will back up files on your account. You will have to apply the knowledge that you acquired in the *Introduction to UNIX and Linux* textbook by John Muster (McGraw-Hill/Osborne, 2002) for writing scripts, copying files, and making directories.

Step 1 If you do not already have directories called *command, html, users, cgi-bin,* and *archive,* please create them now using **mkdir**. You will need to place several files into each directory. In the *html* directory, create several files that end with *.html.* In the *users* directory, create several files that end with *.dat* and *.txt.* Finally, create several *.cgi* files in the *cgi-bin* directory.

You should determine the command(s) needed to copy the files into the *archive* directory. The command must copy all *.txt, .dat, .html,* and *.cgi* files from their respective directories into the appropriate directory. It is helpful to use **cd** to change to the actual directory to copy from before copying the files. Using the absolute path is a good idea.

✖ Warning

Be sure that you use the **cp** command rather than the **mv** command.

Step 2 Go to the *commands* directory.

Step 3 Using your favorite text editor, create a new script called *archive*.

Step 4 Write the commands you determined in the planning section in your script.

Step 5 Using the **chmod** command, make this script executable.

Step 6 Run the script. Change to the *archive* directory and verify that all files have been copied.

✔ Hint

It is a good idea to write and test small portions of the script. Write and verify that you can copy the *.txt* files before trying the *.dat* files. Writing scripts in small chunks helps reduce the frustration associated with scripting and nearly guarantees a working script. This is called sourcing the script.

 10 MINUTES

Lab Exercise 9.03: Setting Permissions on Files and Folders

While you were working on LaTrina's site, you noticed that many of her files had the wrong permissions. You suggest to LaTrina she should modify permissions on several of her files. All files in the *html* and *cgi-bin* directories should be readable and executable. The *archive* directory should allow only the owner of the file to read or modify the archived files. The *user* directory needs the owner and others to read and write the files.

You need to set the permissions on LaTrina's files. This is accomplished using the **chmod** command. **chmod** can change permissions on files and directories. You will need to specify the permission number for each.

> ✖ **Warning**
>
> Setting files at 606 is a bit dangerous. This means that anyone can modify the file, if they know the direct path. Thus, setting *.html* files with the 606 permission is a bad idea. The *.txt* and *.dat* files in the *users* directory are reasonably safe to set with 606. You have written the scripts that maintain these files. A hacker would have to know the exact path to the file to do any damage.
>
> You set 606 because of the manner most web servers handle scripts by default. They run your scripts as the user nobody, which is in the other group. Thus for your scripts to be able to modify the file, they need to allow others to write.

Learning Objectives

In this lab, you will set permissions on files and folders. By the end of this lab, you'll be able to:

- Set permissions for a file
- Set permissions on a directory
- Set permissions recursively

Lab Materials and Setup

The materials you need for this lab are:

- The directories and files created in Lab Exercise 9.02

- Computer with Red Hat Linux 7.3 installed

Getting Down to Business

The following steps will help you set permissions on files and directories. You will have to apply the knowledge that you acquired in the *Introduction to UNIX and Linux* textbook by John Muster (McGraw-Hill/Osborne, 2002) for setting permissions.

✖ Warning

> Try to avoid setting owner permissions at 0. It is often difficult to set them back to a working permission. Typically, you need root account permissions to fix this problem.

Step 1   Change to the *users* directory. Set the permissions on all *.txt* and all *.dat* files using the **chmod** command. The permissions should provide the owner and others with write ability, and the group with no access.

Step 2   Change to the parent directory of *users*. Set the permission on *users*. The *users* directory should provide the owner and others with write ability and the group with no access.

Step 3   Stay in the parent directory of *users*. Using the **chmod -R** command, set the permissions on the *html* and *archive* directories. The *html* directory will have user full control, everyone else will have read and execute. The archive directory will have full control for the owner, and everyone else will have no access.

Step 4   Change to each directory and perform a long listing. Verify that the access permissions have been changed.

 10 MINUTES

Lab Exercise 9.04: Setting the umask

LaTrina will need to set her permissions every day, as new *.txt* and *.dat* files appear. You help her make the directory automatically apply the desired rights. To ensure default permissions, you use the **umask** command. **umask** works by telling UNIX/Linux what permissions you do not want set. Whenever a new file is created in an **umask**ed directory, that file will have the correct permissions. **umask** is easy to use. To set an **umask**, you subtract the desired permission from 777. The resulting number is the **umask**. For example, if you need 644 permission set on a directory, the **umask** is 777 – 644 = 133. You will need to determine the **umask**s based on the permissions you set on the *users* directory in Lab Exercise 9.03.

Learning Objectives

In this lab, you will set a default permission level on your account. By the end of this lab, you'll be able to:

- Set the **umask** to ensure default permissions in a directory

Lab Materials and Setup

The materials you need for this lab are:

- The directories and files created in Lab Exercise 9.02
- Computer with Red Hat Linux 7.3 installed

Getting Down to Business

The following steps will set a default permission on your directories. You will have to apply the knowledge that you acquired in the *Introduction to UNIX and Linux* textbook by John Muster (McGraw-Hill/Osborne, 2002) for working with **umask**.

Step 1   Determine the appropriate **umask** and write it in the space provided.

_____

_____

Step 2   Set the appropriate **umask**.

Step 3   Change to the *users* directory. Create a file at random and perform a long listing. Ensure that the permission is set correctly.

Lab Analysis Test

1. If you set a directory to mode 644, and a file in the directory to 666, what happens if a member of your group tries to write to the file?

2. Describe how **umask** works.

3. You receive an e-mail from your local administrator. He suggests that for your web pages to run correctly, you need to set the pages to permissions 777. How can you immediately tell that this e-mail is not from your administrator?

4. Which do you prefer: setting permissions using the numbers or the letter arguments? Why?

5. How can you delete a file that you own but do not have write permission for?

Key Term Quiz

Use the following vocabulary terms to complete the sentences below. Not all of the terms will be used.

1

2

4

chmod

directory

execute

file

permission

r

-R

read

umask

w

write

x

1. The command to set permissions on a file is _____.

2. The command to set up the default permissions on an account is _____.

3. The numeric equivalent for the write permission is _____ and the letter argument is _____.

4. When you set a 1 permission, you are allowing a user to _____ the file.

5. The _____ switch will set the mode on all files and subfolders.

Lab Wrap-Up

You have set file permissions that enable a web site to run while also protecting important files. You used **chmod** to set permissions on several files and directories. The **umask** command ensured that new *.txt* and *.dat* files generated by the user will be given the proper permissions.

Solutions

In this section, you'll find solutions to the Lab Exercises.

Lab Solution 9.01

The following steps allow you to translate to and from numeric permissions to a description of the permission:

Step 1

Permission	Owner	Group	Other
777	read, write, execute	read, write, execute	read, write, execute
644	read, write	read	read
640	read, write	read	nothing
751	read, write, execute	read, execute	execute
711	read, write, execute	execute	execute
700	read, write, execute	nothing	nothing

Step 2

Need	Numeric Equivalent
Owner can read and write, group can read and write, other cannot do anything	660
Owner can read, write, and execute; group and other can execute	711
Owner can read and write, group can read, other can read and write	645
Owner can read and write, group and other can read	644

Lab Solution 9.02

The following steps will create the **archive** script:

Step 1   You should have created the necessary files and directories before continuing on with the solution. You should have executed the command **mkdir** *html cgi-bin users archive* to create the directories. Using **touch** *a.html b.html c.html*, you should have created several HTML files. The same command should have been run to create the *.txt*, *.dat*, and *.cgi* files. Be sure you created the files in the proper directory. HTML files should have been created in the *html* directory. The *cgi-bin* directory should hold all *.cgi* files; *users* should hold the *.txt* and *.dat* files.

Step 2   You should have changed to the *command* directory using the command **cd ~/commands**.

Step 3   You should have created the text file with the **pico** *archive* command.

Step 4   You should have entered the following code, then saved and exited the file.

clear

echo *"Copying html files now..."*

cd *~/html*

cp **.html ~/archive*

echo *"Copying cgi files now..."*

cd *~/cgi-bin*

cp **.cgi ~/archive*

echo *"Copying txt files now..."*

cd *~/users*

cp **.txt ~/archive*

echo *"Copying dat files now..."*

cp **.txt ~/archive*

echo *"All files copied, have a nice day!"*

Step 5   You should have made the file executable with the command **chmod 755** *archive*. 755 means that the owner can read, write, and execute, while the rest of the world can read and execute.

Step 6   You should have tested your command several times.

Lab Solution 9.03

The following steps will set the desired permissions for your directories:

Step 1   You should have changed to the *users* directory with the **cd** *users* command. You should then have set the permissions on the *.txt* files so the owner and others can read and write, using the command **chmod 606** **.txt*. You should have set the same permissions on the *.dat* files.

Step 2   You should have changed to the parent directory of *users* with **cd ...** You should have then set the 606 permission on the *users* directory with **chmod 606** *users*.

Step 3   For the *html* and *cgi-bin* directories, you should have executed the command **chmod -R 755** *html cgi-bin*. For the **archive** directory, you should have executed **chmod -R 600** *archive*.

Step 4   You should have used **cd** to change to the *html* directory. You should then have executed the command **ls -l** to verify that the files have the proper settings of **rwxr-xr-x**.

Lab Solution 9.04

The following steps will set the **umask**:

Step 1   The desired permission for the *users* directory is 606. Performing the subtraction 777 − 606 should have resulted in 171.

Step 2   You should have set this **umask** with the command **umask 171**.

Step 3   You should have created a file using **touch**. You should have then used **ls -l** to verify that the owner and other have **rw** access.

Chapter 10

Controlling User Processes

Lab Exercises

In the previous chapters, you created several jobs. Every UNIX/ Linux command becomes a job. In this chapter, you will learn how to manage these jobs. You will learn how to list the running jobs for yourself and all users. In addition you will learn how to kill, suspend, and reactivate jobs for yourself and other users. Finally, you will learn how to keep a job running even after you log out of the system.

20 MINUTES

Lab Exercise 10.01: Listing Running Jobs

Jeff needs to learn how to watch what his employees are doing on the system. He also needs to kill jobs he finds undesirable. Finally, he has a piece of software that he needs to run all the time, even when he is logged out. Your mission is to help Jeff resolve his problems using UNIX.

You will show Jeff how to master the multitasking features of UNIX. These features allow users to work with multiple commands. The feature is a bit clunky when compared to Windows, but does work well once you are familiar with the keystrokes.

After teaching Jeff the basics of UNIX, you start on his first problem: listing the jobs on the system. The **ps** utility is reasonably complex and has several switches, some of which are not listed in **man**. You start by teaching Jeff to list his processes, and then gradually move up to listing processes of various individual users.

✔ **Hint**

This lab works best on a system with multiple users running processes. If you are working on a standalone system, create several users and switch to them. To switch to users, log in as one user. Then use the command **su** *username* to switch to the user called *username*. Perform this action several times before completing the lab.

Learning Objectives

In this lab, you will list the processes on the system. By the end of this lab, you'll be able to:

- List your processes
- List processes of all users on the system
- List processes of specific users on the system

Lab Materials and Setup

The materials you need for this lab are:

- Computer with Red Hat Linux 7.3 installed

Getting Down to Business

The following steps will guide you in listing the various switches required when using the **ps** utility and running the **ps** command to perform the required actions. You will have to apply the knowledge that you acquired in the *Introduction to UNIX and Linux* textbook by John Muster (McGraw-Hill/Osborne, 2002) for listing user processes.

Step 1 You will need to determine the switches needed to perform the following tasks. Please write them in the space provided.

Desired Output	ps Switch Needed
All processes	_____
User details about the process	_____
Specific user processes	_____
All user processes	_____
Running commands only	_____

Step 2 List all of your processes.

_____

_____

Step 3   List all processes and user details for your account.

_____

_____

Step 4   List all processes for users.

_____

_____

Step 5   List all processes for users and user details.

_____

_____

Step 6   List all processes and their details for an individual user.

_____

_____

Step 7   List all processes running for all users.

_____

_____

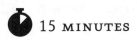 15 MINUTES

Lab Exercise 10.02: Terminating Jobs

Jeff has had some experience with programs that crash or become unstable. He needs to know how to terminate these processes. The command to terminate processes is **kill**. As you are aware of by now, the **kill** command, along with the appropriate switch, sends a signal to the process that tells it to terminate. By default, the **kill** command sends a software terminate signal, which tells the program to stop running. When using the **kill** command in conjunction with the **-9** switch, the **-9** switch has the license to kill any command. Be wary of using **-9** because it will stop *all* processes, and not let the process clean up after itself or gracefully shut down. Thus if a process opened a file, and it was killed with a **-9**, the file may not be closed properly and the data that was changed in the file will be permanently lost.

In this lab, you will practice using the **kill** command to stop other commands that you have started. To prepare for the lab, you will start several commands and place them in the background. Once the commands are in the background, you will terminate the process. You will need to run through the **kill** switches until you find one that terminates the command. Run **ps** to both get the process ID (PID) to kill and to verify that the utility was terminated.

Learning Objectives

In this lab, you will place jobs in the background and terminate jobs. By the end of this lab, you'll be able to:

- Kill your own processes
- Place jobs in the background

Lab Materials and Setup

The materials you need for this lab are:

- Computer with Red Hat Linux 7.3 installed

Getting Down to Business

The following steps will guide you in starting several commands to gain practice killing commands. You will have to apply the knowledge that you acquired in the *Introduction to UNIX and Linux* textbook by John Muster (McGraw-Hill/Osborne, 2002) for terminating commands.

Step 1   To practice the **kill** command, you need several commands in memory. You will start three commands and place them in the background. Execute the following commands:

man ls &

pico &

sleep 60000 &

✔ **Hint**

Placing an & after a command will run the job in the background.

Step 2   Kill the **sleep** command.

Step 3   Kill the **pico** command.

Step 4   Kill the **man** command.

Step 5   After each **kill** command is executed, run **ps** to verify that the command was terminated.

 10 MINUTES

Lab Exercise 10.03: Suspending and Activating Jobs

Jeff understands how to list his processes and terminate jobs. However, he would like to learn how to temporarily stop jobs. Often, he is working in **vi** and needs to copy a file from another directory. Currently, he saves his work, quits **vi**, copies the file, then restarts **vi**. He would like to do this faster. You will show Jeff how to place the current job in the background.

You will start a **vi** session, and then send it to the background. While working with the editor, you will practice multitasking with UNIX/Linux by temporarily suspending the job and running a shell command.

Learning Objectives

In this lab, you will start a **vi** session and place the session in the background to allow you to copy a file. By the end of this lab, you'll be able to:

- Place the current job in the background
- Bring a background process to the foreground

Lab Materials and Setup

The materials you need for this lab are:

- Computer with Red Hat Linux 7.3 installed

Getting Down to Business

The following steps guide you in using the multi-tasking features of UNIX. You will have to apply the knowledge that you acquired in the *Introduction to UNIX and Linux* textbook by John Muster (McGraw-Hill/Osborne, 2002) for suspending and reactivating commands.

Step 1   Start a **vi** session.

Step 2   Place the job in the background.

Step 3   What keystroke sent the job to the background?

_____

_____

Step 4   Verify that the command is still running. What is its status?

_____

_____

Step 5   Copy the file **passwd** from the **/etc** directory to your home directory.

Step 6   Bring the session to the foreground.

 15 MINUTES

Lab Exercise 10.04: Terminating Jobs for Other Users

Jeff has noticed that one of his employees is playing a game on company time. Jeff would like to end the game whenever he notices it running. He knows that **kill** can do the trick, but he cannot seem to kill the other user's processes.

You tell him that **kill** is the correct command. However, he needs to be logged into the UNIX server with **root** permissions. Once logged in as **root**, he can kill user processes at will. You will need to create a couple of running processes. Once this is done, you will log in as **root** and kill these jobs.

✔ Hint

The scenario described above is typical in an organization with one UNIX/Linux server controlling other UNIX/Linux workstations. The lab is designed to work on a workstation that you have root permissions on.

Learning Objectives

In this lab, you will kill processes of other students. By the end of this lab, you'll be able to:

- Kill jobs of other users

- Log on as **root** using the **su** (substitute user) command

Lab Materials and Setup

The materials you need for this lab are:

- Computer with Red Hat Linux 7.3 installed

- The **root** password

> ✔ **Hint**
>
> If you are on a standalone UNIX computer, you can use the **su** command to log in as several users. As each user, start a program that you wish to kill.

Getting Down to Business

The following steps will guide you in terminating processes of other users. You will have to apply the knowledge that you acquired in the *Introduction to UNIX and Linux* textbook by John Muster (McGraw-Hill/Osborne, 2002) for listing and killing user processes.

> ✖ **Warning**
>
> If you are given **root** access to a UNIX computer that other users share, do not abuse your **root** privileges. Abusing **root** privileges can be cause for dismissal from school or work.

Be advised that the **root** account is all-powerful. It has the power to do anything on a UNIX/Linux computer, including deleting the operating system. If you are unsure of a command while logged in as **root**, do not run it.

Step 1 Log in to your system. Place a job in the background. Switch users to another account. Create another process in the background.

> ✔ **Hint**
>
> Recall that the **su** command will allow you to switch to another user without logging out.

Step 2 Use the **su** command to login as **root**.

Step 3 Get the PID for the process you wish to kill.

Step 4 Kill the PID.

Step 5 Run **ps** to verify that the command is no longer running.

 20 MINUTES

Lab Exercise 10.05: Using nohup **to Run Processes After Logging Out**

LaTrina has another question. She needs a program on the web site to run all the time. Currently, the only way she knows to keep the programming running is to stay logged in. She knows it is possible for a regular (non-**root**) account to specify that a command runs in the background, after the user logs out. A command to solve this problem is the **nohup** command. **nohup** will keep a program running even after you log out. **nohup** is short for "no hangup." The syntax is **nohup** *command* **&**.

✔ Tip

The **nohup** command originated when users needed modems to connect to a UNIX computer. To save on costs, **nohup** allowed the users to dial in, start a process, disconnect, and reconnect several hours later when the process should have completed. **nohup** has stuck around despite the reduced dependency on dial-in accounts.

Learning Objectives

In this lab, you will use **nohup** to keep a command running after logging out. By the end of this lab, you'll be able to:

- Compile a C++ program
- Use the **nohup** command

Lab Materials and Setup

The materials you need for this lab are:

- Computer with Red Hat Linux 7.3 installed
- A C++ compiler, or the compiled version of **runforever.exe**.

✔ **Hint**

The compiled version of **runforever.exe** can be found at **www.osborne.com**. Search for this text and follow the **Downloads For This Book** link.

Getting Down to Business

The following steps will guide you in running a program using the **nohup** command. You will have to apply the knowledge that you acquired in the *Introduction to UNIX and Linux* textbook by John Muster (McGraw-Hill/Osborne, 2002) for using **nohup**.

If you do not have access to the compiled version of **runforever.exe**, you will need to create it. Create a text file called *runforever.cpp* with the following code. Run the command **c++ -o runforever.exe** *runforever.cpp*. When you have entered the code correctly, **runforever.exe** will execute. Nothing will appear on the screen.

```
#include <iostream.h>

void main()

{

    int x = 7;

    while(x <= 7);

}
```

Step 1   Create or acquire the program **runforever.exe**.

Step 2   Use **nohup** and the **&** to execute **runforever.exe**.

Step 3   Log out and log back in as another user. List all user processes. **runforever.exe** should be running. If desired, kill the job by logging back in as the user that created the process and use the **kill** command.

✖ **Warning**

If you are using a shared UNIX implementation, you should kill the job after you are finished. Most system administrators consider leaving useless programs in RAM quite rude.

Lab Analysis Test

1. Once you determine a PID for a process, how do you terminate it?

_____

_____

2. How do you determine a PID for the user *jsmith*?

_____

_____

3. Suppose you have three commands in the background. How can you bring the second command to the foreground, but leave the other two in the background?

_____

_____

4. Why should you use the **-9** option as a last resort?

_____

_____

5. How can a boss use **ps** to determine who works the hardest?

_____

_____

Key Term Quiz

Use the following vocabulary terms to complete the sentences below. Not all of the terms will be used.

%

&

-1

-15

-2

-9

c++

CTRL-Z

fg

kill

nohup

ps

1. The _____ utility will keep a program running even after the user logs out.

2. The _____ signal is the default for **kill**.

3. To place commands in the background, you can use the _____ when starting the command or _____ during the execution of the command.

4. To get the PID of a job, use the _____ command.

5. To bring a job to the foreground, use the _____ utility.

Lab Wrap-Up

The multitasking features of Linux, while easy to work with, pale in comparison to Windows. You learned how to use **ps** to get the job information for both your jobs and those of the entire system. You then used **kill** to eliminate a running utility. Finally, you used the **nohup** command to place a command in RAM, running essentially forever.

Solutions

In this section, you'll find solutions to the Lab Exercises.

Lab Solution 10.01

The following steps allow you to create and kill processes:

Step 1   The correct switches needed for **ps** are displayed in the table.

Desired Output	ps Switch Needed
All processes **root** and users	**-A**, **-e**, or **aux**
User details about the process	**u**
Specific user processes	**-u** *username*
All user processes	**au**
Running commands only	**-r**

To solve the problems, you needed to use **ps** and a variety of switches. Figures 10-1 through 10-3 show typical output.

Step 2   You should have executed **ps** to list your processes.

Step 3   You should have executed **ps u** to list details about your processes. Figure 10-1 displays output for **ps** and **ps u**.

Step 4   You should have executed **ps -A | more** to list all user processes. Figure 10-2 shows sample output of the **ps -A** command.

Step 5   You should have executed **ps -A u** to list user details for all user processes.

Step 6   You should have executed **ps u -au** *bob*, where *bob* is the username, to see processes and details for any job related to *bob*. Your output should be similar to Figure 10-3.

Step 7   You should have executed **ps -A r** to see running processes for all users.

> ✔ **Hint**
>
> There are several undocumented **ps** switches. The switches **j**, **l**, **s**, and **t** all provide different output, and are probably not listed in your man pages. Try them and discover what they do.

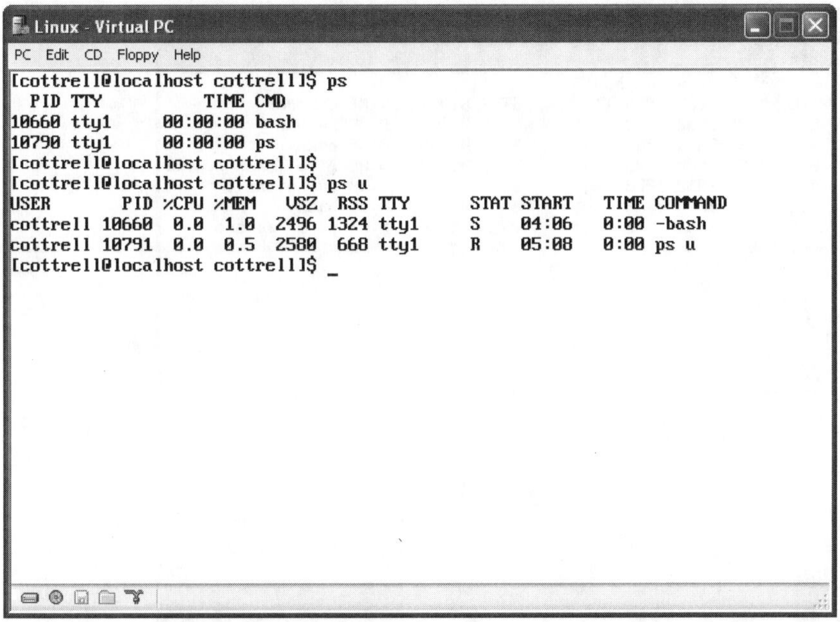

FIGURE 10-1 Output for ps and ps u

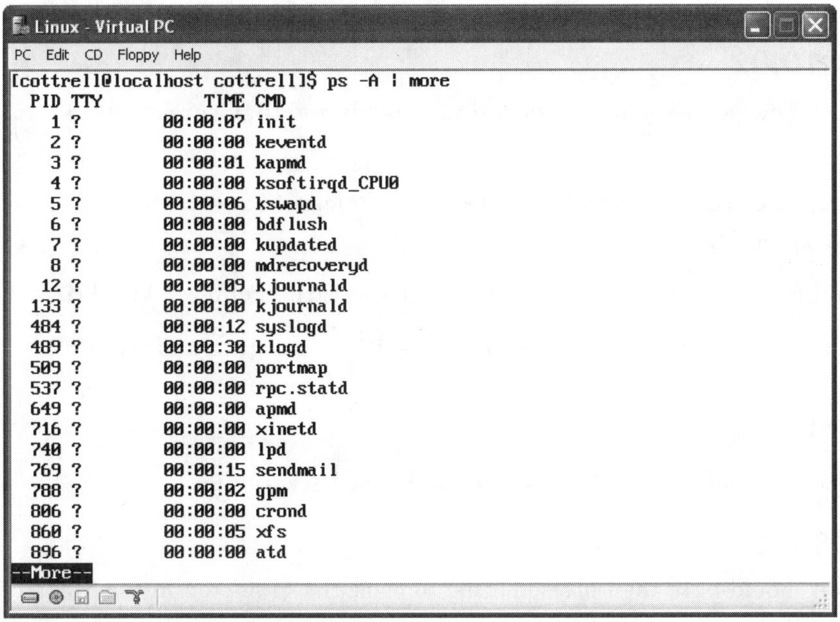

FIGURE 10-2 Output for ps -A | more

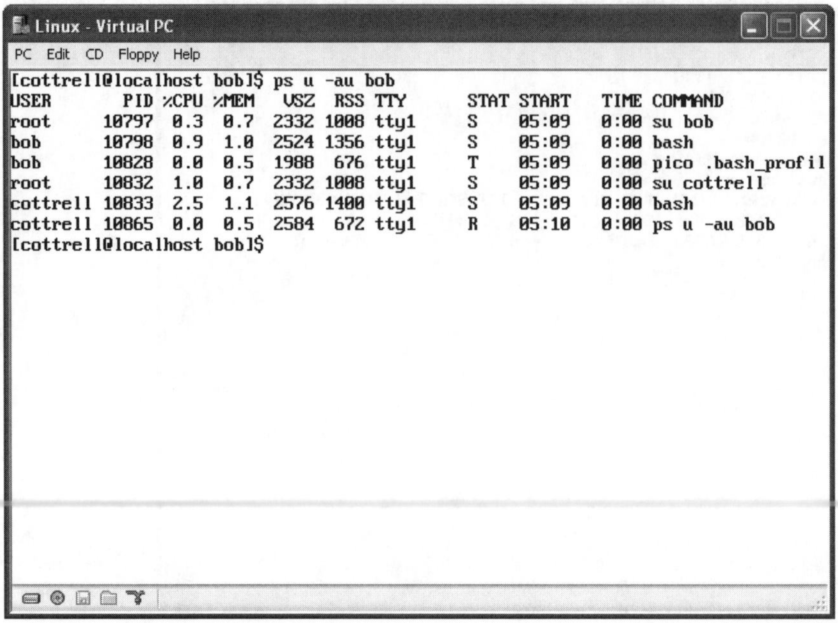

FIGURE 10-3 Output for **ps u -au** *bob*

Lab Solution 10.02

The following steps allow you to generate several commands and then subsequently terminate them:

Step 1 You should have executed **man ls &**, **pico &**, and **sleep 60000 &** to place three processes in the background.

Step 2 You should have executed **ps** to get the PID for **sleep**, then entered **kill PID**.

Steps 3 and 4 You should have executed **ps** to get the PIDs, then entered **kill -9 PID**.

Lab Solution 10.03

The following steps allow you to practice placing jobs in the background:

Step 1 You should have executed **vi hello**.

Steps 2 and 3 You should have then pressed CTRL-Z to place the **vi** session in the background.

Step 4 You should have run **ps u** to see the commands. As shown in Figure 10-4, the **vi** session should be listed with the status of **T**.

```
Linux - Virtual PC
PC  Edit  CD  Floppy  Help
[cottrell@localhost cottrell]$ ps u
USER       PID %CPU %MEM   USZ  RSS TTY       STAT START   TIME COMMAND
cottrell 10660  0.0  1.0  2496 1344 tty1      S    04:06   0:01 -bash
cottrell 10879  2.8  1.7  4944 2156 tty1      T    05:12   0:00 vim hello
cottrell 10882  0.0  0.5  2580  668 tty1      R    05:12   0:00 ps u
[cottrell@localhost cottrell]$ _
```

FIGURE 10-4 A stopped job

Step 5   You should have executed **cp /etc/passwd ~**.

Step 6   You should have run **fg** to bring the **vi** session to the foreground.

Lab Solution 10.04

The following steps allow you to kill jobs of other users:

Step 1   You should have logged in to the system as a regular user.

Step 2   You should have created a **vi** process and placed it in the background using CTRL-Z.

Step 3   To kill the process, you should have first switched to **root** using **su root**. You should have entered the password when indicated. You should have found the PID by using **ps -A u**, then killed the process using **kill -9** 21396. (You should have used your PID instead of the PID listed.)

Step 4   You should have run **ps u** to verify that the process is indeed terminated.

Lab Solution 10.05

The steps on the following page allow you to run a command after logging out.

Step 1   You should have logged in to the system as a regular user. Using **pico** or your favorite text editor, you should have created the *runforever.cpp* file. You should then have compiled it and created the **runforever.exe** program with the command **c++ -o runforever.exe** *runforever.cpp*.

Step 2   Once the program was working, you should have executed **nohup runforever.exe &**. A file called **nohup.out** should have been created.

Step 3   You should have logged out of the system and then logged back in. You should have listed all processes with the **ps -A u** command. You should then have verified that **runforever.exe** was still running, and, if desired, killed the job.

Chapter 11

Managing, Printing, and Archiving Large Files

Lab Exercises

In the last chapter, you worked with permissions and a script. In this chapter, you will learn how to manipulate how files are stored on the system. You will compress files to save space. You will work with floppy disks and splitting files to fit on floppy disks. You will use the **root** permissions to stop undesired user permissions. Finally, you will use **pr** to format a document for printing.

 20 MINUTES

Lab Exercise 11.01: Compressing a File

Jeff has some problems with files and disk space. He would like you to help him manage the files on his system. He needs to learn how to use less space and send files to disk for storage. In addition, he is having trouble printing his documents. You know several utilities that can help Jeff with his problem. You begin by teaching Jeff how to compress files, then move on to accessing a floppy disk.

Jeff mentioned that his UNIX system is running out of disk space. You have determined that he has several large files which he says are important but rarely used. You will help Jeff compress these rarely used files, using the commands **gzip** and **tar**. **gzip** is similar to the PC's **pkzip** format. It does a very nice job compressing files. **tar** allows you to place several files into one file for easy transport and storage. It can be thought of as a box that holds several files.

Learning Objectives

In this lab, you will use UNIX compression utilities. By the end of this lab, you'll be able to:

- Compress a file using **gzip** and **compress**

- Uncompress a file using **unzip** and **uncompress**

- Condense files using **tar**

- Compress files using **tar**

Lab Materials and Setup

The materials you need for this lab are:

- Computer with Red Hat Linux 7.3 installed

Getting Down to Business

The following steps allow you to compress files using **gzip**, **gunzip**, and **tar**. You will have to apply the knowledge that you acquired in the *Introduction to UNIX and Linux* textbook by John Muster (McGraw-Hill/Osborne, 2002) for compressing files.

Step 1 Create a directory called *chapter11*. Copy all of the *.conf* files from the */etc* directory. If this directory is invalid or protected, your instructor may provide a different set of files to work with.

COMPRESSION

Step 1 What is the size of the *pine.conf* file?

_____

_____

Step 2 Compress this file using the **compress** utility. What is its size now?

_____

_____

Step 3 Uncompress this file using the **uncompress** utility.

Step 4 Compress this file using the **gzip** utility. What is its size now?

_____

_____

Step 5 Uncompress this file using the **gunzip** utility.

TARRING

Step 1   List all the files that begin with s and end with *.conf*. Total their sizes. What is their total size? How many files did you list?

_____

_____

Step 2   Create a new **tar** file called *sconf.tar*. Add the files you found in Step 1.

Step 3   What is the size of the *sconf.tar* file? Why is it bigger?

_____

_____

Step 4   Delete this archive. Rebuild the archive using the **gzip** option for **tar**.

Step 5   What is the size of the *sconf.tar* file?

_____

_____

🕐 20 MINUTES

Lab Exercise 11.02: Saving Files to Disk

Jeff, like most business managers, does some work at home. Currently, he is unable to move his files to and from his house. He has resorted to printing the files, hand-writing the changes on the output, and coding the change the next day. This is extremely inefficient, as well as being costly. Jeff wants to be able to take the files home and work on his home computer. A catch: he prefers to work on his Windows computer, rather than his Linux computer. He wants to know how his files can transfer from UNIX to Windows.

✔ **Hint**

DOS disks are readable in Windows systems.

You know that most Linux and UNIX systems allow the copying of files to and from a DOS disk. UNIX provides a suite of utilities called **mtools**, which provide for the formatting and accessing of DOS disks.

Learning Objectives

In this lab, you will use the **mtools** suite for Linux. By the end of this lab, you'll be able to:

- Format a floppy disk for use in both UNIX and Windows
- List the files on a disk
- Copy files to the disk
- Delete files on the disk

Lab Materials and Setup

The materials you need for this lab are:

- Computer with Red Hat Linux 7.3 installed
- The *chapter11* directory created in Lab Exercise 11.01

- A floppy disk that can be erased

- Physical access to the floppy drive on the UNIX/Linux computer

- Physical access to a Windows-based PC that has Notepad installed on it

✔ **Hint**

Any text editor on a PC will work. In addition, Macintosh computers can read and write DOS disks as well.

Getting Down to Business

The following steps will allow you to copy files to and from DOS disks. You will have to apply the knowledge that you acquired in the *Introduction to UNIX and Linux* textbook by John Muster (McGraw-Hill/Osborne, 2002) for working with the **mtools** utilities.

Step 1 Format the floppy disk. Use the **-f** parameter and the appropriate size.

Step 2 Copy all files in the *chapter11* directory that begin with k, l, or m to the floppy drive.

Step 3 List the files on the floppy drive and verify that all copied.

Step 4 Remove the files on the floppy drive that begin with m. Verify that the files were deleted.

Step 5 Take the disk to a Windows computer. Open several of the files in Notepad. Make a change to one of the files. Be sure the filename does not have the *.txt* extension.

Step 6 Go back to the UNIX computer and copy the file you changed to the *chapter11* directory. Verify that the file can still be read and that the change is present.

 10 MINUTES

Lab Exercise 11.03: Splitting a Large File

Jeff needs to get a file to his home computer. However, the file is quite large and will not fit on a floppy disk. He needs to split the file into pieces. The file will be taken home to his home computer and edited in pieces.

You will use the **split** command to break the file into pieces. To allow Jeff to edit the file, you will limit the size of the output file to 1.2 million bytes. This may seem large, but it is just a little smaller than the size of a high-density floppy disk. By limiting the size to 1.2 million bytes, Jeff can add about 200,000 characters to each file and easily rebuild the file at work.

Learning Objectives

In this lab, you will split one large file into several smaller files. By the end of this lab, you'll be able to:

- Split and rejoin files

Lab Materials and Setup

The materials you need for this lab are:

- Computer with Red Hat Linux 7.3 installed
- The *chapter11* directory created in Lab Exercise 11.01
- At least three floppy disks that can be erased
- Physical access to the floppy drive on the UNIX computer

Getting Down to Business

The following steps will help you split large files. You will have to apply the knowledge that you acquired in the *Introduction to UNIX and Linux* textbook by John Muster (McGraw-Hill/ Osborne, 2002) for working with the **split** utility.

Step 1   Navigate to the *chapter11* directory. Create a large text file with repeated uses of the following command: **cat *.conf >>** *big.file*. Continue to append to the file until it is about 3 million bytes.

Step 2   What is the length of *big.file?*

_____

_____

Step 3   Split the file into several pieces, each no more than 1,200,000 bytes. Use the base name (prefix) of *big.*

Step 4   List the files created. Sum their sizes and verify that the total is the same as the size of *big.file.*

_____

_____

Step 5   Copy each file to a floppy disk.

Step 6   Delete *big.file.*

Step 7   Make a change to one of the files (preferably the first file).

Step 8   Copy the three files from the floppy drive back to the *chapter11* directory.

Step 9   Rebuild the file. Verify that it is the correct size.

 20 MINUTES

Lab Exercise 11.04: Removing Files by Owner

Jeff has had to fire an employee named Bob. Bob was not happy about being fired, so he played some tricks on the UNIX/Linux system before he left. He left several files in other users' directories that contain rude and inappropriate images and words. Jeff wants to remove these files. As he is considering legal action, he needs to save the files for the lawyers while removing the files for the users' sake. One big problem is the permissions. Bob set the files with 755, allowing everyone read and execute ability, while denying the users the ability to delete the files.

Jeff knows that **root** can delete the file, but he doesn't want to look in every user's directory for a "bob" file. He asks if there is a way to search the entire disk structure by user name. To help Jeff solve his problem, you teach him the finer points of the **find** command.

Learning Objectives

In this lab, you will place a few files on your partner's home directory. Your partner will then find these files and remove them. By the end of this lab, you'll be able to:

- Use the **find** command to locate files by user name

- Delete files by user name

Lab Materials and Setup

The materials you need for this lab are:

- Computer with Red Hat Linux 7.3 installed

- Access to the **root** account

- Two normal user accounts

✔ Hint

This is a good lab to run with a partner. Partner A can set his directory permissions to **rwx**, to allow partner B to place a file in his directory. Partner A can then search for the files as **root**, deleting those he sees fit. If partners are impossible, create an account that will take the place of partner B.

Getting Down to Business

The following steps will help you place a few files in user accounts and then find them with the **find** command. You will have to apply the knowledge that you acquired in the *Introduction to UNIX and Linux* textbook by John Muster (McGraw-Hill/Osborne, 2002) for working with the **find** utility.

Step 1   Log in as partner A. Change to the parent directory of your home directory. Record the current permission settings. Set your directory to have the **rwx** permissions.

Step 2   Partner B will now create a few files and save them in partner A's directory.

Step 3   Log in as *root*.

Step 4   Run the **find** command that finds all files by partner A. Use the parent directory of your home directory as the starting point.

Step 5   Use the **exec** switch to **cat** the files into a file called *bobfiles*. Include the directories in the output.

Step 6   Use the **ok** switch of **find** to remove files by partner A. **ok** is similar to **exec**, except you will be prompted for approval before action.

Step 7   Verify that all files created by partner B are gone from partner A's directory. Partner A should now set the permissions back to their original state.

 20 MINUTES

Lab Exercise 11.05: Formatting a Document for Printing

Jeff maintains a phone list of his employees. As it changes, he prints it for his employees. He prefers a two-column output, sorted across the columns, rather than down the columns. He wants a heading that reads *September Phone List* and includes the page number. He asks how to do this in UNIX/Linux.

This procedure is easy in Word, but UNIX/Linux is a little trickier. You will need to use the **sort** command, redirected into the **pr** command, then redirected into the **lp** command. The really tricky part is the **pr** command. Here you need several switches to generate the correct output.

You will spend the bulk of your time learning how to use **pr**. Once the **pr** is correct, you will redirect the **sort** into the **pr**. Finally, when the output is correct, you will redirect to a printer of your choice.

✔ **Tip**

Consult the man pages for **pr** to determine the proper switches.

Learning Objectives

In this lab, you print a formatted document. By the end of this lab, you'll be able to:

- Use **pr** to format output
- Use **lp** to print to a printer
- Chain redirect output

Lab Materials and Setup

The materials you need for this lab are:

- Computer with Red Hat Linux 7.3 installed
- A file containing first names and phone numbers
- (Optional) Access to a printer

Getting Down to Business

The following steps guide you in using **pr** to format a file. You will have to apply the knowledge that you acquired in the *Introduction to UNIX and Linux* textbook by John Muster (McGraw-Hill/Osborne, 2002) for using **pr**.

✔ **Hint**

By default, your UNIX/Linux computer will print to one of several possible printers. Most likely, the first entry in the **/etc/printcap** will be used. If you need to change printers, you will need to use the **-P** switch for **lp**. For example, if you wanted to print to the LaserJet4 printer, you would use the **lp -P** *LaserJet4* command.

If you do not have a printer, simply use the **more** command in place of the **lp** command.

Step 1 Create a file called *phonelist* using the following data:

bob 999-5555	debbi 111-1111
carole 999-6666	laurie 222-2222
adam 777-8888	heather 333-3333
joyce 999-9999	lise 444-4444
bev 999-0000	steve 555-5555
bob 999-1111	joanne 666-6666
tom 999-2222	linda 777-7777
art 999-3333	barb 888-8888
rose 999-4444	amy 999-9999
robert 999-7777	

Step 2 Use **pr** to prepare the file for printing.

Step 3 Add the switch to create two columns. What switch is needed?

_____

_____

Step 4 Add the switch to change the heading to *Phone List*. What switch is needed? What portion of the header is changed?

_____

_____

Step 5 Add the switch to change the date to *September*. What switch is needed?

_____

_____

Step 6 Add the switch to double space the output. What switch is needed?

_____

_____

Step 7 Sort the file and redirect it into the complete **pr** command.

Step 8 Add the switch to the **pr** command to sort across columns. What switch is needed?

_____

_____

Step 9 Redirect the entire command to the **lp** command.

Lab Analysis Test

1. Which does a better job of compressing a file: **gzip** or **compress**?

    _____

    _____

2. What happens to the file size if you **gzip** a file compressed with **compress**? To determine this, **compress** the file. Rename the file back to the original name without the .Z extension, then compress with **gzip**.

    _____

    _____

3. Jeff has several **tar** files on his account. One is named *feather.tar*. How can Jeff display the contents of *feather.tar*?

    _____

    _____

4. Why did the developers of Linux provide the ability to read disks formatted in Windows, while Microsoft provided no utility to read disks formatted by Linux?

    _____

    _____

5. You used **find** to determine the files changed by the installation of an application. How can this action be considered unethical?

    _____

    _____

Key Term Quiz

Use the following vocabulary terms to complete the sentences below. Not all of the terms will be used.

cat

compress

find

gunzip

gzip

lp

pr

sort

split

tar

uncompress

1. The _____ utility will create a file holding several other files.

2. To prepare a document for printing, including page numbers and headers, you can use the _____ utility.

3. To break a large file into several smaller files, the _____ utility is useful.

4. The _____ utility provides a new file having the extension of .Z.

5. To search the computer for a file, you would use the _____ command.

Lab Wrap-Up

You compressed files on an account to save space and learned how to take files home on a floppy disk. These files were modifiable on a Windows computer. Files that were too large to fit on floppy disks were broken into the proper size chunks with the **split** command. Reassembling them was simply a matter of using the **cat** command. You helped Jeff remove the traces of a disgruntled employee. Finally, you helped him create nice output from his UNIX computer.

Solutions

In this section, you'll find solutions to the Lab Exercises.

Lab Solution 11.01

The following steps allow you to practice using the compression utilities on a UNIX/Linux system:

Step 1 You should have created the directory with **mkdir** *chapter11*, then changed to the directory with the command **cd** *chapter11*. You should have copied the desired files with the command **cp /etc/*.conf ..** You should then have listed the files to verify that the files were copied.

COMPRESSION

Step 1 To determine the size of *pine.conf*, you should have entered **ls -l pine.conf**. On a test system, for example, the size is 14,566 bytes.

Step 2 You should have compressed the file with **compress *pine.conf***. After compression, the size on the above test system was 7,512 bytes.

Step 3 You should have uncompressed the file with the command **uncompress *pine.conf***.

Step 4 To compress with **gzip**, you should have run **gzip *pine.conf***.

Step 5 After **gzip**ping the file, the size on the test system was 5,010 bytes.

Step 6 **gunzip** will unzip this file. The command you should have used is **gunzip *pine.conf***.

TARRING

Step 1 To list the files, you should have entered **ls -l s*.conf**. Figure 11-1 shows the three files on the test system. Their total size is 1,303 bytes.

Step 2 To create the archive, you should have entered the command **tar -c -f *sconf.tar* s*.conf**. The **-c** switch creates a new archive. **-f** creates the file called *sconf.tar*. **s*.conf** is the list of files to include. Alternatively, you could have listed the three files instead of the wildcard command.

Step 3 The size of the *.tar* archive is 10,240 bytes. It is bigger because the **tar** command adds information to the file about directory and file listing.

```
linux - Virtual PC                                                    _ □ ✕
PC  Edit  CD  Floppy  Help
[cottrell@localhost chapter13]$ mdir a:
 Volume in drive A has no label
 Volume Serial Number is 7B24-545A
Directory for A:/

KRB~1     CON      2281 09-08-2002   16:32   krb.conf
KRB5~1    CON       640 09-08-2002   16:32   krb5.conf
LDSO~1    CON        98 09-08-2002   16:32   ld.so.conf
LDAP~1    CON      6198 09-08-2002   16:32   ldap.conf
LIBUSE~1 CON       2295 09-08-2002   16:32   libuser.conf
LOGROT~1 CON        505 09-08-2002   16:32   logrotate.conf
LPD~1     CON     18802 09-08-2002   16:32   lpd.conf
LTRACE~1 CON       5803 09-08-2002   16:32   ltrace.conf
MODULE~1 CON         51 09-08-2002   16:32   modules.conf
MTOOLS~1 CON       1913 09-08-2002   16:32   mtools.conf
        10 files                38 586 bytes
                             1 416 192 bytes free

[cottrell@localhost chapter13]$
```

FIGURE 11-1 Files that begin with s

Step 4 You should have deleted the archive with **rm *sconf.tar*.** You should then have used **man tar** to get the switch for using **gzip** in a **tar** archive. Most likely, the switch was **-z**. To **tar** and **compress**, you should have executed the command **tar -c -f *sconf.tar* -z s*.conf.**

Step 5 Using **tar** and **compress** on the files should have created an archive the size of 858 bytes.

Lab Solution 11.02

The following steps allow you to use the **mtools** utilities provided by UNIX:

Step 1 You should have acquired a 3.5-inch floppy disk that you can copy files to and determined the type of the disk. If it has two holes at the top, it is a high-density (HD) disk. Disks with one hole are double-density (DD) disks. Most likely, you have a HD disk. To format the HD disk, you should have entered the command **mformat -f 1440 a:**. To format the DD disk, you should have entered the command **mformat -f 720 a:**.

Step 2 You should have copied the files with a variant on the command **mcopy [klm]*.conf a:**.

```
linux - Virtual PC
PC   Edit   CD   Floppy   Help
[cottrell@localhost chapter13]$ mdir a:
 Volume in drive A has no label
 Volume Serial Number is 7B24-545A
Directory for A:/

KRB~1     CON      2281 09-08-2002   16:32   krb.conf
KRB5~1    CON       640 09-08-2002   16:32   krb5.conf
LDSO~1    CON        98 09-08-2002   16:32   ld.so.conf
LDAP~1    CON      6198 09-08-2002   16:32   ldap.conf
LIBUSE~1 CON       2295 09-08-2002   16:32   libuser.conf
LOGROT~1 CON        505 09-08-2002   16:32   logrotate.conf
LPD~1     CON     18802 09-08-2002   16:32   lpd.conf
LTRACE~1 CON       5803 09-08-2002   16:32   ltrace.conf
MODULE~1 CON         51 09-08-2002   16:32   modules.conf
MTOOLS~1 CON       1913 09-08-2002   16:32   mtools.conf
        10 files             38 586 bytes
                          1 416 192 bytes free

[cottrell@localhost chapter13]$
```

FIGURE 11-2 Output of **mdir**

Step 3   To verify the files copied, you should have entered **mdir a:**. Your files should be listed. Figure 11-2 shows the output for **mdir**.

Step 4   You should have deleted the files with the command **mdel m*.conf a:**. Again, you should have used the **mdir a:** command to verify that the files have been deleted.

Step 5   To test the disk, you should have logged off of your UNIX computer and gone to any Windows computer. You should have started Notepad or another text editor, and opened any *.conf* file on the A drive. Figure 11-3 shows *ldap.conf* opened in Notepad.

Step 6   You should have gone back to your UNIX computer and logged back in. You should have then changed to the *chapter11* directory with the **cd** *chapter11* command. You should have copied the file from the A drive to the current directory with the command **mcopy a:ldap.conf ..** You should have pressed **y** if prompted to overwrite the file, and used **more** to show the file. Figure 11-4 verifies that the name Lee Cottrell was added to the file.

FIGURE 11-3 *ldap.conf* in Notepad on an XP computer

FIGURE 11-4 *ldap.conf* on the Linux computer

Lab Solution 11.03

The following steps allow you to create and split a large file:

Step 1 You should have changed to the *chapter11* directory with the **cd ~/chapter11** command. You should have then created *big.file* using the **cat *.conf >> big.file** command, running it about 10 times to get to the required byte size.

Step 2 You should have then determined the length of the file with **ls -l** *big.file*. The length of the test file was 3,624,120 bytes.

Step 3 You should have split the file into chunks of at most 1.2 million bytes, each file having *big* as part of the name. A command that would work is **split -C 1200000** *big.file big*. Figure 11-5 shows the result of this command.

Step 4 You should have then listed the files with **ls**.

Step 5 You should have copied the files to floppy disks with repeated uses of the **mcopy** command. To copy the first file, you should have entered **mcopy** *bigaa* **a:**, and then repeated for all files created.

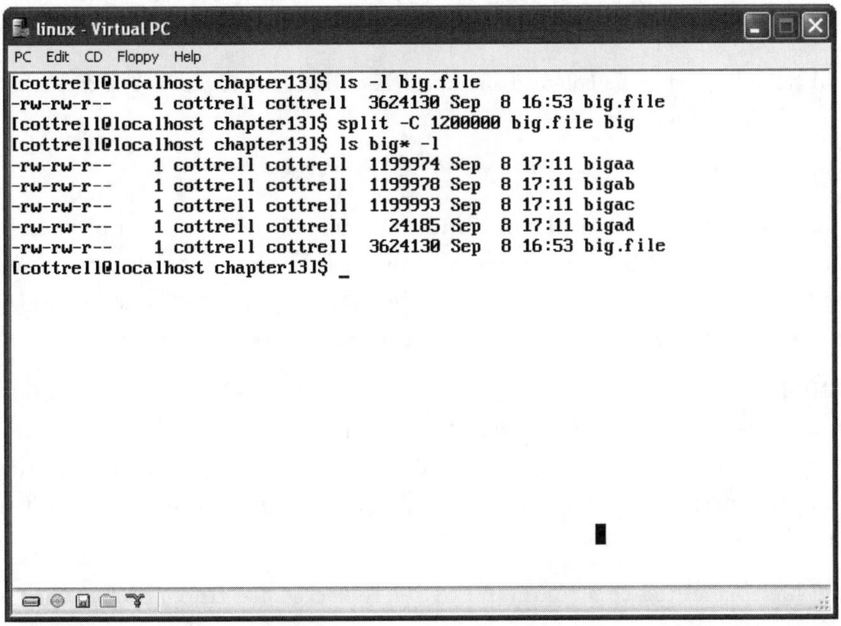

Figure 11-5 Files created with the **split** command

Step 6   You should have deleted *big.file* with **rm** *big.file*.

Step 7   You should have used **pico** to change one of the files. Alternatively, you could have changed the file on a Windows computer using Notepad. For example, you could have added your name to the first file.

Step 8   To rebuild the file, you should have used **cat**, which displays the contents of a file. When redirected to another file, it can act as a copy command. The command **cp big* >>** *big.file* should have been used to rebuild your file.

Step 9   You should have verified that the size of the rebuilt *big.file* is slightly larger than the original *big.file*. It is larger because you added some text to the file.

Lab Solution 11.04

The following steps should help you place a few files in user accounts and then find them with the **find** command. The users for the example are *cottrell* and *bob*. *cottrell* is partner A, and *bob* is partner B.

Step 1   You should have logged in as *cottrell* and navigated to the parent of your home directory with the **cd ..** command. Using pencil and paper, you should have recorded your settings. You should then have used **chmod 777** *cottrell* to set the permissions on your directory.

Step 2   You should have logged in as *bob* and saved a file called *hacked.file* in the *cottrell* directory. You should then have logged out.

Step 3   You should have logged in as **root**.

Step 4   You should have entered the **find** command that started in the parent of your home directory. It should have searched by user to find all files by *bob*. A command that will work is **find /home -user** *bob* **-print**. If you got error messages, modify the command by adding **2> errorfind** to the command. You should see *hacked.file* in the *cottrell* directory.

Step 5   Once the **find** command was working, you should have added the **-exec** switch to the command. To store the files, you could have used the **cat** command and redirection to store the files for future reference. The following command will create a file called *bobfiles*, and include the file contents and the directory the file was stored in: **find /home -user** *bob* **-exec cat {} \; -print >** *bobfiles*.

Step 6   You should have executed this command to delete *hacked.file*: **find /home -user** *bob* **-ok rm {} \;**, pressing **y** to delete the appropriate file. Figure 11-6 shows the output of the **find** command.

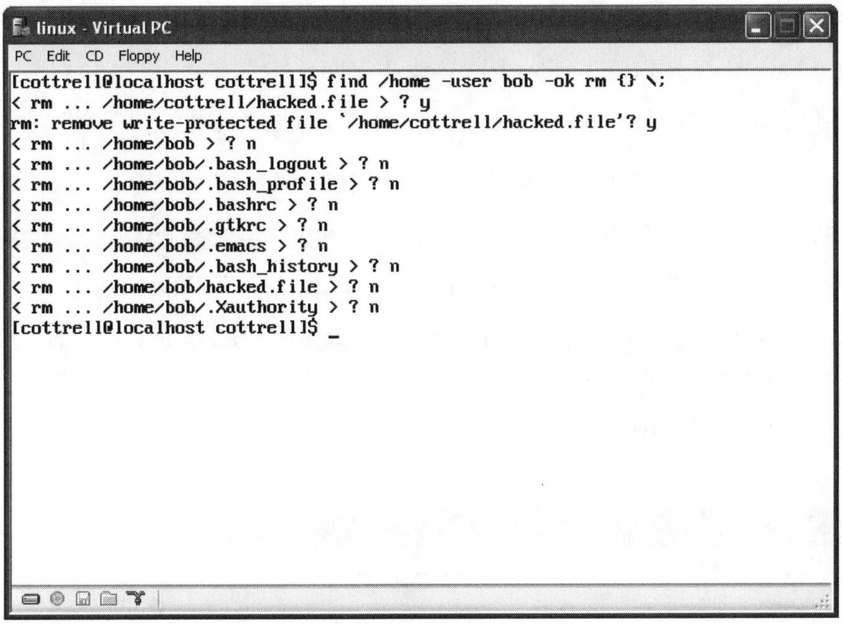

FIGURE 11-6 Output of the **find** command

Step 7 You should have logged in as *cottrell* and listed the files in the directory to determine that *hacked.file* is gone.

✖ Warning

Be careful using **rm** with **find**. Since you are logged in as **root**, you can delete all of Bob's files. If Bob has several files in his directory, you can modify the **find** to start searching in the */home/cottrell* directory.

Lab Solution 11.05

Step 1 Using **vi**, **pico**, or another text editor, you should have created a file called *phonelist*, with at least 10 names and numbers in the list.

Step 2 You should have used the **pr** utility to prepare the document for printing. Entering **pr** *phonelist* should have created a document with one column and the default headings.

Step 3   You should have used the **-2** switch to force two columns.

Step 4   You should have changed the header by using **-h** *'Phone List'*.

Step 5   You should have changed the date by using the **-D'***September***'** switch.

Step 6   To double-space the output, you should have used the **-d** switch.

Step 7   Forcing the output to sort across instead of down should have been done with **-a**.

Step 8   The entire **pr** command is **sort** *phonelist* **| pr -a -2 -D'***Sept***' -d -h** *'Phone List'*.

Step 9   You should have redirected the **pr** command into the **lp** utility. The entire command follows. The output of the command can be seen in Figure 11-7.

   sort *phonelist* **| pr -a -2 -D'***September***' -d -h** *'Phone List'* **| lp**

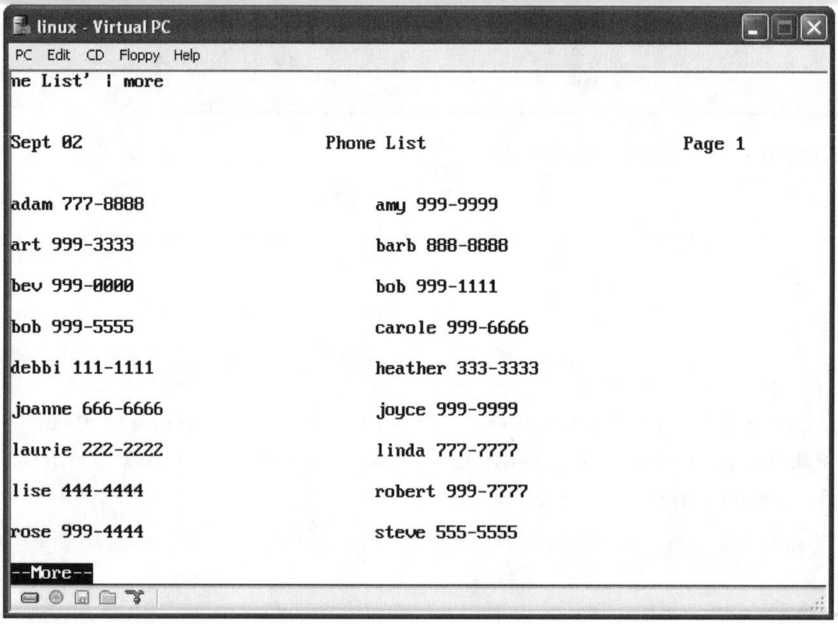

FIGURE 11-7 Output of the **pr** command

Chapter 12

Accessing and Touring Graphical Desktops

Lab Exercises

In previous chapters, you worked with the command line. You learned the traditional UNIX/Linux interface. In this chapter, you will work with the GUI capabilities of UNIX. UNIX/Linux uses variants of the X Window System (X11) program to provide GUI functionality for the user.

You will use the Gnome version of the X Window System. Gnome was installed by default in your Linux installation. In this chapter, you will perform basic file management tasks. You will learn to customize you desktop settings. This includes background images and links. Finally, you will configure your computer to connect to the Internet.

 20 MINUTES

Lab Exercise 12.01: Performing File Management Tasks

Jeff likes the stable operating system that UNIX provides, but he dislikes the command-line interface. He wants to use UNIX with a graphical user interface (GUI), like Windows. He feels if Linux had a viable GUI, he could use it as a primary OS in the company, and save the company millions in software costs.

You decide to teach Jeff how to use the X Window System implementation that is on his computer. You will show him how to manipulate his files, change his desktop settings, run some built-in applications, and create separate desktops.

You will start Jeff's exploration of the X Window System interface with some file management techniques. You will show him how to rename files, copy files and directories, delete files, and utilize the trashcan. The skills are similar to those used in a Windows interface, so Jeff should catch on quickly.

Learning Objectives

In this lab, you will use the X Window System to manage files. By the end of this lab, you'll be able to:

- Start the X Window System interface on your UNIX system

- Start Nautilus or another file manager

- Copy, rename, and delete files and directories

Lab Materials and Setup

The materials you need for this lab are:

- Computer with Red Hat Linux 7.3 installed

- A version of the X Window System installed on your computer

Getting Down to Business

The following steps will help you perform basic file management techniques in Gnome. You will have to apply the knowledge that you acquired in the *Introduction to UNIX and Linux* textbook by John Muster (McGraw-Hill/Osborne, 2002) for using Gnome.

Step 1   Create a directory called *xpractice*. In this directory, create three text files called *x1*, *x2*, and *x3*. Feel free to use **touch** or copy other files. Also, place a *.jpg* or other image file onto a floppy disk. This file will be used in this and other exercises.

Step 2   Start the X Window System interface on your system.

Step 3   Start the file management system.

Step 4   Rename the directory called *xpractice* to *xname*.

Step 5   Copy the file **/etc/lpd.conf** to the *xname* directory.

Step 6   Delete the files *x1*, *x2*, and *x3*.

Step 7   Change the file permissions on **lpd.conf** to full control for the owner, and everyone else read and execute.

Step 8   Move an image file from the floppy disk to your home directory.

 15 MINUTES

Lab Exercise 12.02: Customizing the Desktop

Jeff likes Gnome. However, he enjoys modifying his desktop and feels that the default blue background is boring. He also wants to know how to add links to the desktop, like in Windows. You assure Jeff that he can modify his desktop and computer as much as he wants. You will show him how to set a wallpaper, add icons to the desktop and panel, and configure a screen saver.

✔ **Hint**

The panel in Gnome is equivalent to the Start button in Windows. The panel button looks like a foot on your desktop.

Learning Objectives

In this lab, you will customize your Gnome desktop. By the end of this lab, you'll be able to:

- Change the wallpaper on your desktop
- Add icons to the desktop and panel
- Configure a screen saver

Lab Materials and Setup

The materials you need for this lab are:

- Computer with Red Hat Linux 7.3 installed
- An image file to be used as the desktop
- Any text file or program on your home directory

Getting Down to Business

The following steps will help you customize the desktop. You will have to apply the knowledge that you acquired in the *Introduction to UNIX and Linux* textbook by John Muster (McGraw-Hill/Osborne, 2002) for working with Gnome.

Step 1 Right-click the desktop to change your background image.

Step 2 Choose a screen saver from the Settings menu on the panel.

Step 3 Add a link to your panel to a file in your home directory.

Step 4 Add a link on your desktop to a file in your home directory.

 45 MINUTES

Lab Exercise 12.03: Using Included Gnome Applications

Linux as the primary OS is starting to look possible. Jeff wants to know if Linux can replace the three most popular functions performed by his staff: word processing, spreadsheet analysis, and graphic manipulation. You tell Jeff that Linux has a word processor called AbiWord, a spreadsheet program called Gnumeric, and GIMP (GNU Image Manipulation Program). You will show Jeff how to use these tools to create a letter and modify an image.

✔ **Hint**

StarOffice is a free office suite program available from **www.sun.com**. It performs most of the same functions as Microsoft Office.

Learning Objectives

In this lab, you will perform several common office tasks. By the end of this lab, you'll be able to:

- Start programs from the panel
- Use AbiWord to create a simple letter
- Use Gnumeric to create a simple budget sheet
- Use GIMP to modify a picture

Lab Materials and Setup

The materials you need for this lab are:

- Computer with Red Hat Linux 7.3 installed
- The image you copied in Lab Exercise 12.01
- The AbiWord, Gnumeric, and GIMP programs installed
- (Optional) A printer installed on your computer

✔ **Hint**

A default installation of Red Hat 7.3 with Gnome should include these packages. If your installation does not include any of the applications, you will need to insert your Red Hat CD to reinstall.

Getting Down to Business

The following steps will help you create a simple letter in AbiWord, build a budget in Gnumeric, and apply a filter to your image. You will have to apply the knowledge that you acquired in the *Introduction to UNIX and Linux* textbook by John Muster (McGraw-Hill/Osborne, 2002) for using the Gnome applications.

Use AbiWord

Step 1 Start AbiWord from the panel. It is located under the Programs | Applications panels.

Step 2 Create a cover letter for a job application. Please follow the proper letter standards as recommended by your school.

Step 3 Print your letter.

Use Gnumeric

Step 1 Start Gnumeric from the panel. It is located under the Programs | Applications panels.

Step 2 Create a budget sheet for your current income and expenses. You should list all incomes and total them. You should then list all expenses and total them. Finally, calculate the money left over by subtracting total expenses from the total incomes.

Step 3 Print your budget.

Use GIMP

Step 1 Start GIMP from the panel. It is located under the Programs | Graphics panels.

Step 2 Apply a filter to the image. Choose a filter that is quite obvious when it is applied.

Step 3 Place your name in the image.

Step 4 Print your image.

 10 MINUTES

Lab Exercise 12.04: Configuring the Internet Settings

Jeff is convinced that Linux can be used as a primary operating system. He decides to test Linux on his computer before making the switch. He installs Linux without a hitch, and everything is fine until he attempts to connect to the Internet. Nothing happens. You know that Linux, despite its simple installation, is not configured for the Internet out of the box. You will need to configure Linux to connect.

✔ **Tip**

Consult the *Introduction to UNIX and Linux* textbook for instructions on installing Red Hat Linux 7.3.

Learning Objectives

In this lab, you will connect your computer to the Internet. By the end of this lab, you'll be able to:

- Start the Internet connection tool
- Configure Linux to use a proxy server to access the Internet

✔ **Hint**

A proxy server is a computer that allows other computers to connect to the Internet. Proxy servers allow an organization to both control access to the Internet and protect their user computers.

Lab Materials and Setup

The materials you need for this lab are:

- Computer with Red Hat Linux 7.3 installed

- Access to the Internet

- The IP address of your school's proxy server

- The **root** password for the computer

✔ **Hint**

If you do not know your proxy or do not have a proxy, you can still complete this lab. Unfortunately, you will not be able to connect to the Internet.

Getting Down to Business

The following steps will help you connect your computer to the Internet using a proxy server. You will have to apply the knowledge that you acquired in the *Introduction to UNIX and Linux* textbook by John Muster (McGraw-Hill/Osborne, 2002) for working with Gnome.

✔ **Hint**

You will need to get the address of the proxy server and the ports that it serves. Your instructor or system administrator should know these numbers. If you do not have an address, use 127.0.0.1 as the proxy and 80 as the port. This is the loopback address. Using this number will not connect you to the Internet, but will not interfere with your school's network.

Step 1 Start the Internet Configuration Wizard.

Step 2 Enter the **root** password when prompted.

Step 3 Create a new Ethernet connection. Use DHCP unless your instructor tells you differently.

Step 4 Start Netscape Communicator. Set the connection preferences for the proxy server to point to your school's proxy server. The proxy settings are under the Advanced Preferences.

Lab Analysis Test

1. You have managed files with both the X Window System and the command-line interface. Which do you prefer using? Why?

_____

_____

2. If you want to copy a file from the **/etc** directory to your home directory, which is faster: copying the file in the command-line interface, or copying the file in the GUI? Why?

_____

_____

3. What are three differences you see between the X Window System and the version of Windows you are familiar with?

_____

_____

4. How can Linux both reduce the costs for computer ownership and have productive users immediately after the install?

_____

_____

5. Why does the X Window System call the items in the panel and on the desktop "links" instead of "shortcuts"?

_____

_____

Key Term Quiz

Use the following vocabulary terms to complete the sentences below. Not all of the terms will be used.

AviWord

desktop

DHCP

favorites

GIMP

Gnome

Gnumeric

links

panel

port

proxy

1. The _____ is equivalent to the Windows Start button.

2. To create or change a picture, you can use the _____ software.

3. A _____ shares an Internet connection.

4. The _____ menu is the only place on the panel you can add links.

5. The program _____ is equivalent to MS Excel.

Lab Wrap-Up

You have completed the tour of the X Window System. You learned how to customize both your desktop and the panel with custom pictures and links. You also used three powerful applications to solve three common business problems. You wrote a letter in AbiWord, created a budget in Gnumeric, and applied a filter to an image using GIMP. Finally, you configured your Linux computer to use a proxy server to access the Internet.

Solutions

In this section, you'll find solutions to the Lab Exercises.

✔ **Hint**

> The following directions are for the Gnome GUI. Gnome is the default GUI installed on a Red Hat Linux installation.

Lab Solution 12.01

The following steps allow you to use the Nautilus file manager system in the Gnome IDE:

Step 1   You should have created the directory called *xpractice* with **mkdir** *xpractice*, then changed to this directory with **cd** *xpractice*. You should have created *x1*, *x2*, and *x3* using the **touch** command. You should have executed **touch** *x1 x2 x3*.

Step 2   You should have started the X Window System with the **startx** command. After a short pause, the Gnome desktop should have been displayed.

Step 3   You should have started the Nautilus file management system by right-clicking the home icon, and selecting the Open menu entry. The Nautilus shell should have appeared, as shown in Figure 12-1. The icons and their meanings should have been obvious.

Step 4   Most of the steps to use Gnome are right-clicks. To rename the *xpractice* directory, you should have right-clicked the directory and selected Rename. Then you should have typed the new name and pressed ENTER. You should have opened *xname* by right-clicking it and selecting Open or by double-clicking it.

Step 5   To browse to a different directory, you should have either typed the path in the address bar or used the arrow buttons on the toolbar to move around. Except for long paths, it is much easier to type the path. You should have typed **/etc** into the address bar, then used **find** to locate the file called **lpd.conf**. You should have right-clicked **lpd.conf** and selected Copy File. A fast way to jump to the file is to click in the File area and type the first letter, in this case *l*. You should have browsed back to your *xname* directory by entering **~/xname** in the address bar. Then you should have right-clicked any white area on your screen and selected Paste Files. The file should have been copied.

FIGURE 12-1 The Nautilus shell

Step 6   To delete the files, you should have sent them to the trashcan. You should have selected each file you wanted to delete. To select multiple files, you can CTRL-click as in Windows. You should have clicked the *x1* file, then held down CTRL on your keyboard and clicked the other files to delete. You should have sent them to the trashcan by right-clicking any selected file and choosing Move To Trash. Your trashcan icon should now have papers spilling out of it as shown in Figure 12-2. To empty the trash, select the File menu in Nautilus, and select Empty Trash. Click Empty to permanently remove the files from your system.

Step 7   To change the permissions in the **lpd.conf** file, you should have right-clicked the file and selected Properties from the menu. In the Properties window, you should have selected the Permissions tab. You should then have set the permissions to 755, or **-rwxr-xr-x**. As shown in Figure 12-3, you should have checked the desired boxes.

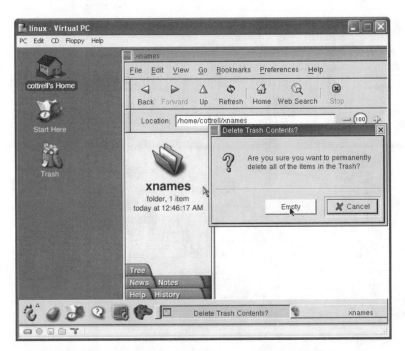

FIGURE 12-2 Emptying the trash

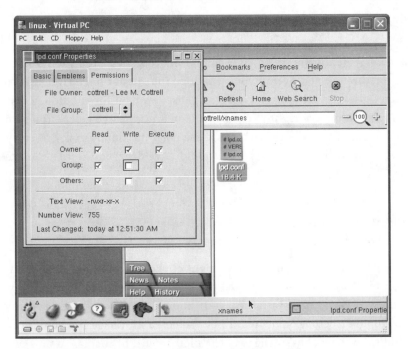

FIGURE 12-3 Changing file permissions

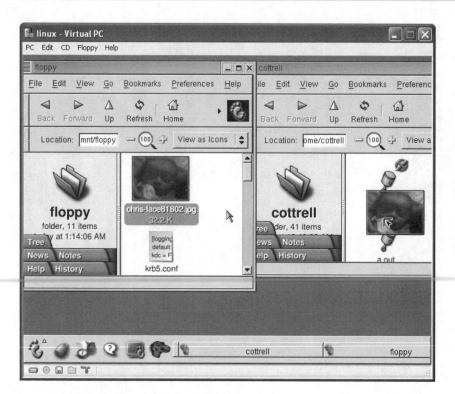

Figure 12-4 Moving a file from a floppy disk

Step 8   You needed to access the disk drive in your computer. Your first step should have been to provide an icon for the floppy drive on your desktop. You should have right-clicked on the desktop and selected Disks | Floppy. After a slight pause, an icon for the floppy disk should have appeared. You should have right-clicked this icon and selected Open. You should have arranged your windows on the screen so you could see both the floppy disk directory and the home directory. As shown in Figure 12-4, you should have dragged the file from the floppy disk to your home directory.

Lab Solution 12.02

The following steps allow you to customize your desktop:

Step 1   To change your background, you should have right-clicked the desktop and selected Change Desktop Background. You should have clicked the Browse button and browsed to your home directory. On a standard Red Hat installation, your home directory will be in **/home/**yourusername. From your home directory, you should have selected an image file you liked as a background. You should then have chosen the way the picture will be displayed on the

FIGURE 12-5 Setting a background picture

desktop. The tiled option covers the desktop with repeated images. The centered option places the image in the center of your desktop, with the desktop color around the image. The scaled options attempt to stretch the picture to fit your screen. Figure 12-5 shows a background with a centered picture. You should have clicked OK to finish the configuration.

Step 2 To change your screen saver, you needed to access the panel. You should have selected the panel (the foot button) | Programs | Settings | Desktop | Screen Saver. You should then have selected the desired screen saver from the list. A demonstration of the screen saver was shown. You should have configured the delay for the screen saver and, if desired, selected a password for the screen saver. This setting requires the user to enter a password before resuming the session. Only use this if you are the sole user of a UNIX computer. When you were finished, you should have clicked OK.

Step 3 To modify your panel, you should have added icons to the Favorites directory. You should have right-clicked the foot button and selected Edit Menus. The Gnome menu editor

should have appeared. You should have selected the Favorites menu on the left edge of your
screen, then clicked New Item to create a new shortcut. You should then have named your
shortcut and entered a description for the shortcut. The description will appear as a tool tip
when the mouse hovers over the shortcut. You should have entered the command to run. You
should then have selected the type of link, the application link being the most common. Finally
if desired, you should have selected an icon for your shortcut. Figure 12-6 depicts the shortcut to
a.out. You should have clicked the Save button, then exited out when finished creating icons.

Step 4   To create a shortcut on your desktop, you should have opened Nautilus by right-
clicking the home icon and selecting Open. You should have browsed to the file or application you wished to shortcut from the desktop. You should have right-clicked and dragged the
icon to the desktop. If you did this correctly, the menu shown in Figure 12-7 should have
appeared. You should have selected Link here to build the shortcut. A new icon with an
arrow in the upper-right corner appeared. This is the link to the program.

Figure 12-6 Creating a shortcut on the panel

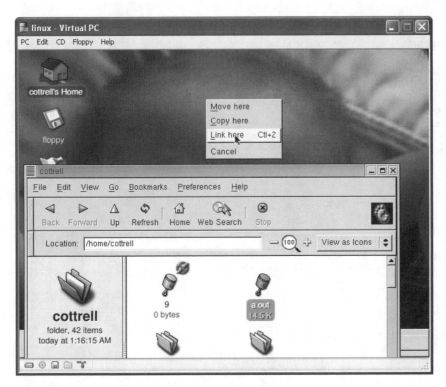

FIGURE 12-7 Creating a shortcut on the desktop

Lab Solution 12.03

The following steps allow you to use AbiWord, Gnumeric, and GIMP:

Step 1 You should have started AbiWord by selecting the panel | Programs | Applications | AbiWord. You should have typed your letter in the document and then saved the document as *coverletter* by clicking on the disk button. You should have spell checked the document using the spell check button (the button shows ABC and a green check mark). You should then have printed the document with File | Print.

Step 2 You should have started Gnumeric by selecting the panel | Programs | Applications | Gnumeric. In cell A1, you should have entered your name, and then proceeded to fill in your budget items. Use the following table as a guide.

	A	B
1	Lee M. Cottrell	
2	Monthly Income	4500

	A	B
3	Rent Income	1500
4	Total Income	=b2 + B3
5		
6	Expenses	
7	Mortgage	1300
8	Gas	160
9	Food	450
10	Electricity	95
11	Entertainment	450
12	Cable	70
13	School Loan	350
14	Car Loan	500
15	Total Expenses	=sum(b7:b14)
16		
17	Left Over	=b4 − b15

Step 3 You should have started GIMP by selecting panel | Programs | Graphics | The GIMP. In GIMP, you should have selected File | Open, then browsed to the picture and double-clicked to open it. You should have right-clicked the image and selected Filter to see the list of filters. You should have picked any filter. The Artistic | Cubist filter would have been a good choice. You should then have clicked the T tool on the toolbox, and clicked inside the image to create a text region. In the dialog box that appeared, you should have selected the desired font and typed your name. You should have right-clicked and selected Save to save the document, then right-clicked and selected Print.

Lab Solution 12.04

The following steps allow you to connect to the Internet through a proxy server:

Step 1 You should have started the Internet Connection Wizard by selecting panel | System | Internet Connection Wizard.

Step 2 You should have entered the **root** password when prompted. Linux should have automatically started the Add Device Wizard.

Step 3 You should have selected the Ethernet connection, then clicked OK for the remaining screens. After the device is added, you should have selected the new Ethernet connection and activated it with the Activate button. You should have closed this window.

Step 4 You should have started Netscape Composer from the panel | Programs | Internet | Netscape Communicator. You should have selected Edit | Preferences, then the Advanced tab. You should then have clicked on the Proxies entry and selected the Manual entry. You should have added the proxy address to the FTP and HTTP entries, as shown in Figure 12-8. The other entries can be entered if you have the port assignments. Once these numbers were entered, you should have closed Netscape and reopened it. You should then have been able to access the Internet.

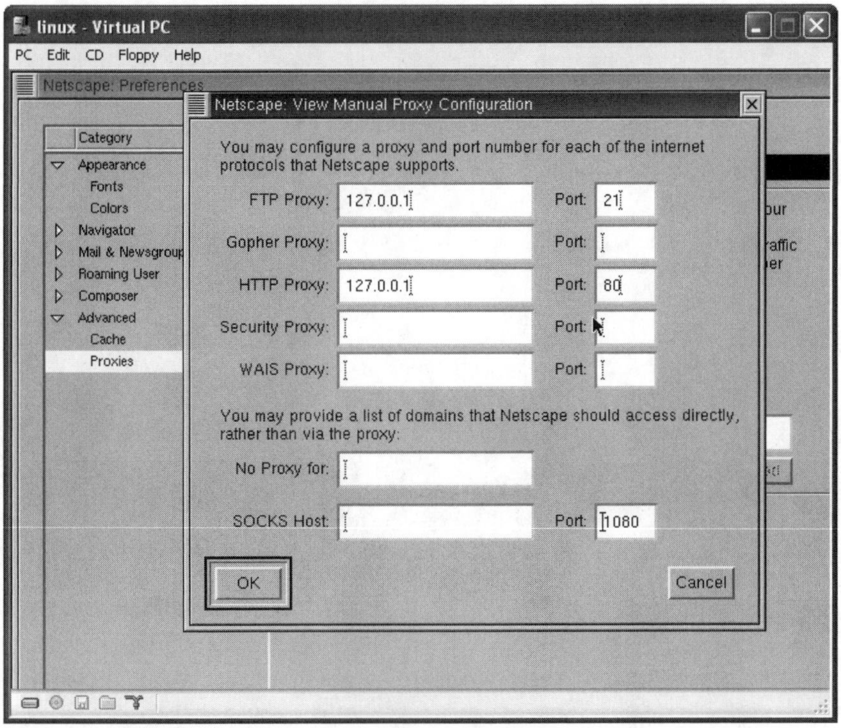

Figure 12-8 Setting proxy information

Chapter 13

Administering a Linux PC System

Lab Exercises

In the previous chapters, you mastered the day-to-day tasks needed by a normal user. In this chapter, you will handle some common administrator tasks. You will shut down the UNIX/Linux computer and manage users. You will create a boot disk in case of disaster. Finally, you will install software on the server.

 15 MINUTES

Lab Exercise 13.01: Shutting Down and Restarting UNIX/Linux

Jeff has decided to move his UNIX/Linux server to his office. This will allow him to quickly solve any problems that arise. He is concerned about how to shut down the server. He figures that simply hitting the power button is bad, and would like to know how to move the server.

Learning Objectives

In this lab, you will shut down the server several times. By the end of this lab, you'll be able to:

- Shut down Linux properly
- Boot Linux using GRUB
- Boot to maintenance mode

Lab Materials and Setup

The materials you need for this lab are:

- Computer with Red Hat Linux 7.3 installed
- Access to the **root** account

Getting Down to Business

The following steps will help you shut down the server. You will have to apply the knowledge that you acquired in the *Introduction to UNIX and Linux* textbook by John Muster (McGraw-Hill/Osborne, 2002) to shut down the server.

✔ **Tip**

You will restart the server several times. The command to down the server is **shutdown**.

Step 1   Down the server for halt, using the **shutdown** command.

Step 2   Boot the server normally.

Step 3   Down the server for reboot.

Step 4   Boot into user maintenance mode.

✔ **Hint**

See **www.redhat.com** for more information. Enter a search for single user mode, and select the first entry, booting single user mode.

Step 5   Reboot the server normally.

 13 MINUTES

Lab Exercise 13.02: Managing User Accounts

Zach and Artie have been hired by Jeff's firm to handle some UNIX/Linux programming. Jeff would like you to create accounts for them. In addition, Zach and Artie will be working together and should be in the same group.

> ✔ **Tip**
>
> The **man** pages for **adduser** will be very helpful in this exercise.

Learning Objectives

In this lab, you will create two new users. By the end of this lab, you'll be able to:

- Create users
- Change user passwords
- Change group membership for users

Lab Materials and Setup

The materials you need for this lab are:

- Computer with Red Hat Linux 7.3 installed
- Access to the **root** account

Getting Down to Business

The following steps will help you use the **adduser**, **passwd**, and **groupadd** commands to create the accounts. You will have to apply the knowledge that you acquired in the *Introduction to UNIX and Linux* textbook by John Muster (McGraw-Hill/Osborne, 2002) for managing users.

✔ **Hint**

The command **useradd** is synonymous with the command **adduser**.

Step 1 Create a group called *unixprog*.

Step 2 Create the accounts *zach* and *artie*. Make them members of the *unixprog* group by using the **-g** option.

Step 3 Change the passwords for *zach* and *artie*.

Step 4 Log in as each user and verify their home directory and group membership.

 20 MINUTES

Lab Exercise 13.03: Solving User Problems

One of the new developers, Zach, was working on a program that added an entry to the *.bash_profile* file. Unfortunately, the program was bad and his *.bash_profile* was deleted. Zach asks if you can get this back.

Artie also needs your help: he accidentally printed a very large binary file and changed the permissions on his home directory to 000. He would like you to fix these problems.

You will solve three common problems. You will resolve Zach's problem with a **cp** command. Artie's two problems require the use of **lpq** to see the contents of the print queue, **lprm** to delete from the queue, and **chmod** to reset permissions on the file.

Learning Objectives

In this lab, you solve common user errors. By the end of this lab, you'll be able to:

- Recover a user's *.bash_profile* file

- Manage the print queue

Lab Materials and Setup

The materials you need for this lab are:

- Computer with Red Hat Linux 7.3 installed

- Access to the **root** account

- The users *artie* and *zach*, created in Lab Exercise 13.02

- The capability to pause the printer

Getting Down to Business

The following steps guide you in solving common user errors. You will have to apply the knowledge that you acquired in the *Introduction to UNIX and Linux* textbook by John Muster (McGraw-Hill/Osborne, 2002) for changing permissions and managing a print queue.

Step 1   You need to set up the computer to have some problems. These steps are merely to allow you to practice solving problems. Pause the printer by either turning it offline or powering it down. Verify that the printer is down by entering the command **lpr /etc/hosts**. Log in as *artie*. Execute the print command **lpr /bin/rpm/** to send a large binary file to the printer. Enter **cd ..** to get to the parent of your home directory. Enter the command **chmod 000** *artie*. Perform a long listing to verify that you have no permissions on the *artie* directory.

Step 2   Log in as **root**.

Step 3   Copy the file **.bash_profile** from the *artie* account to the *zach* account. Using **chown**, change the ownership of the **.bash_profile** to *zach*.

Step 4   Check the print queue. Remove any jobs by *artie*.

Step 5   Change to the **/home** directory. Change the permissions on Artie's directory.

 5 MINUTES

Lab Exercise 13.04: Making a Linux Boot Disk

After moving the server to your office, you are unable to locate the boot disk made when the server was installed. The boot disk allows you to boot the server if the boot partition of your hard drive goes bad. You decide to create a new boot disk.

Learning Objectives

In this lab, you will create a boot disk. By the end of this lab, you'll be able to:

- Make a Linux boot disk

Lab Materials and Setup

The materials you need for this lab are:

- Computer with Red Hat Linux 7.3 installed

- A blank floppy disk

- Access to the **root** account

- The kernel build number for your version of UNIX

Getting Down to Business

The following steps will help you create a boot disk. You will have to apply the knowledge that you acquired in the *Introduction to UNIX and Linux* textbook by John Muster (McGraw-Hill/Osborne, 2002) for building a boot disk.

✔ Hint

Do not execute this command in the GUI. Gnome will automatically mount your drive, making the **mkbootdisk** utility fail. If you are in the command prompt and receive an error stating that the volume is mounted, execute **umount /dev/fdo** to unmount your floppy disk.

Step 1   List the directories in the **/lib/modules** directory. The directory with the highest numbers is your current build.

Step 2   Run the **mkbootdisk** command with the build number. Insert a disk when prompted.

Step 3   Run the **mdir** command to see the Linux boot files. Leave the disk in the drive and reboot the system.

 20 MINUTES

Lab Exercise 13.05: Installing the Apache Web Server

Zach and Artie are writing some web pages and would like a web server to allow testing of the pages. They ask you to install the Apache web server, which comes with Red Hat Linux.

You will install the Apache web server from the Red Hat CD. You will need to mount the drive, then run **rpm** to start the installation process.

Learning Objectives

In this lab, you will install the Apache web server. By the end of this lab, you'll be able to:

- Mount a CD-ROM
- Install Apache from the CD

Lab Materials and Setup

The materials you need for this lab are:

- Computer with Red Hat Linux 7.3 installed
- Access to the **root** account of your UNIX server
- Disk 2 of the Red Hat 7.3 installation CDs

Getting Down to Business

The following steps will help you install the Apache Web Server. You will have to apply the knowledge that you acquired in the *Introduction to UNIX and Linux* textbook by John Muster (McGraw-Hill/Osborne, 2002) for working with the command prompt.

Step 1   Insert the CD and mount the drive.

Step 2   Change to the **RedHat/RPMS** directory on the CD.

Step 3   Install all applications associated with Apache.

Step 4   Point your web browser on a different computer to the IP address of your Linux computer. It should respond with a web page stating "It Worked".

Lab Analysis Test

1. Why is it a bad idea to perform your daily tasks as superuser?

_____

_____

2. Why do you need to mount the CD before installing applications?

_____

_____

3. You gave the users _zach_ and _artie_ the password of `secret`. Most likely, your UNIX installation responded with a BAD password message. Why is this a bad password?

_____

_____

4. What happens if you enter the command **lprm all all**?

_____

_____

5. What is the difference between **su** and **su -**?

_____

_____

Key Term Quiz

Use the following vocabulary terms to complete the sentences below. Not all of the terms will be used.

adduser

chmod

chown

groupadd

lpq

lprm

mkbootdisk

mount

passwd

queue

rpm

su

1. The command to change ownership of a file is _____.

2. The print jobs on UNIX/Linux are stored in a _____.

3. The utility _____ installs new Red Hat packages from the CD.

4. _____ allows you to log in as another user.

5. To see your print jobs waiting to print, use the _____ utility.

Lab Wrap-Up

You have successfully administered a UNIX computer. You learned how to shut down the system and reboot the system. You booted the system into single user mode by modifying the GRUB screen. Two new users were added to the system. You solved two common problems with user accounts, the repair of the *.bash_profile* file and the removal of bad print jobs. Finally, you installed a new package for your Red Hat installation.

Congratulations are in order for completing this text. You worked very hard and learned a great deal about working with UNIX. You should feel proud of your accomplishment. You should also feel able to solve any UNIX task.

Solutions

In this section, you'll find solutions to the Lab Exercises.

Lab Solution 13.01

The following steps allow you to boot and reboot the server in various modes:

Step 1 To shut down the server, you should have used the **shutdown** command. If no one else was logged into the server, you could have shut down immediately. If others were on the system, you should have shut down after at least 30 seconds' warning. You should have determined if anyone is logged in with the **who** command. If *root* was the only person logged in, you should have executed **shutdown -h now**. If others were logged in, you should have executed **shutdown -h 30**.

Step 2 To reboot the server, you should have pressed the power button. If you have installed Linux using GRUB, you should have then picked the desired operating system from the list, and continued. Figure 13-1 provides a typical GRUB screen. If you installed LILO, you should have typed **Linux** at the prompt.

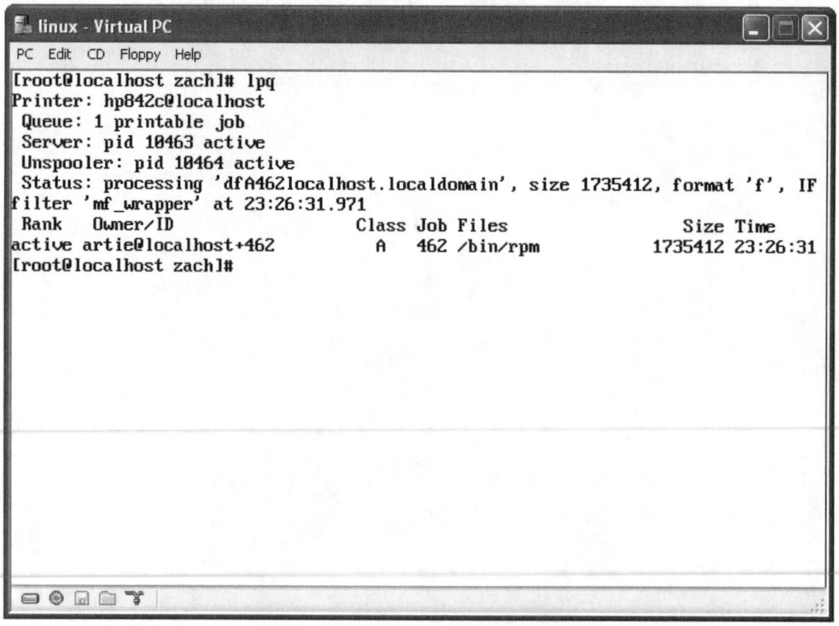

```
linux - Virtual PC
PC  Edit  CD  Floppy  Help
[root@localhost zach]# lpq
Printer: hp842c@localhost
 Queue: 1 printable job
 Server: pid 10463 active
 Unspooler: pid 10464 active
 Status: processing 'dfA462localhost.localdomain', size 1735412, format 'f', IF
filter 'mf_wrapper' at 23:26:31.971
 Rank    Owner/ID              Class Job Files              Size Time
active  artie@localhost+462       A    462 /bin/rpm        1735412 23:26:31
[root@localhost zach]#
```

FIGURE 13-1 Picking an OS in the GRUB screen

Step 3 Rebooting the server uses the **shutdown** command with the **-r** option. You should have entered **shutdown -r** to reboot your computer.

Step 4 Booting into the single user mode is a little tricky in GRUB. At the screen in Figure 13-1, you should have typed **e** to edit your startup options. You should have seen at least three options; you should have then selected the line that starts with **kernel** (it was probably the second line). You should have typed **e** to edit this line, and added the word **single** to the end of the line. Figure 13-2 shows how the line should look. You should have changed nothing except to add **single** to the end of the line. You should have pressed ENTER to save this change, and then typed **b** to boot into single user mode.

Booting into single user mode is much simpler if you are using LILO as your boot manager. In that case, you should have typed **linux single** at the LILO prompt to boot to single user mode.

FIGURE 13-2 Editing the startup line

Step 5 You should have used **shutdown -r now** to reboot the server, and then let the server boot normally.

Lab Solution 13.02

The following steps allow you to create groups in the *unixprog* group:

Step 1 You should have logged in to the system as **root**. You should have then executed the command **groupadd** *unixprog*. This creates the *unixprog* group.

Step 2 You should have built the accounts using the **-g** option. The command **adduser** *artie* **-g** *unixprog* will create the user and make it a member of *unixprog*. You should have created Zach's account after creating Artie's account.

Step 3 Finally, you should have changed their passwords with the **passwd** command. You should have executed **passwd** *artie* to change Artie's password. The password secret is good for now. You should have instructed the users to change their password after they log in.

Step 4 To verify that the accounts were created properly, you should have logged in as each. You should have entered the **pwd** command to check the home directory path. It should be **/home/***artie* or **/home/***zach*. Finally, you should have entered the **groups** command to prove membership in the *unixprog* group.

Lab Solution 13.03

The following steps allow you to fix the problems on the system:

Step 1 No additional commands were needed.

Step 2 You should have logged in as **root** with an **su -** command or a traditional login. You should have changed to Zach's account with the command **cd /home/***zach*. You should have executed **cp ../***artie*/**.bash_profile .** to copy the file from Artie's directory into Zach's directory. You should have performed **ls -a** to verify that the file copied. You should then have made Zach the owner of the file with the command **chown** *zach* **.bash_profile**.

Step 3 To fix Artie's printer problems, you should have stayed logged in as **root** and run the utility **lpq** to see the contents of the print queue. Artie's job should have been listed as in Figure 13-3. You should have removed the job by entering **lprm** *462*, where *462* is the number of the job to delete. You should have then rerun **lpq** to verify that the job is not in the queue and turned the printer back on.

```
[root@localhost zach]# lpq
Printer: hp842c@localhost
 Queue: 1 printable job
 Server: pid 10463 active
 Unspooler: pid 10464 active
 Status: processing 'dfA462localhost.localdomain', size 1735412, format 'f', IF
filter 'mf_wrapper' at 23:26:31.971
 Rank   Owner/ID                 Class Job Files            Size Time
active artie@localhost+462         A   462 /bin/rpm         1735412 23:26:31
[root@localhost zach]#
```

FIGURE 13-3 Output of the **lpq** utility

Step 4 Resetting Artie's directory is an application of the **chmod** command. You should have changed to the parent directory of the *artie* directory with the **cd /home** command. You should have performed **ls -l** to see that Artie's directory is not readable by him. You should have given Artie control over his directory again with the command **chmod 755** *artie*.

Lab Solution 13.04

The following steps allow you to build a boot disk:

Step 1 You should have logged in as *root*. You should have executed **ls /lib/modules** to get the current kernel version. You need this to correctly configure the boot disk. In a default installation of Red Hat 7.3, with no updates installed, you should have build version 2.4.18-3.

Step 2 You should have executed the command **mkbootdisk 2.4.18-3** to build the disk. After waiting for a moment, you should have run **mdir** to see a listing of files. It should be similar to the listing in Figure 13-4.

```
[root@localhost modules]# mdir
 Volume in drive A has no label
 Volume Serial Number is 3D8D-41AE
Directory for A:/

LDLINUX  SYS      6192 09-22-2002   0:06
VMLINUZ       1052336 04-18-2002   7:53  vmlinuz
INITRD   IMG    148043 09-22-2002   0:06  initrd.img
SYSLINUX CFG       122 09-22-2002   0:06  syslinux.cfg
BOOT     MSG       203 09-22-2002   0:06  boot.msg
         5 files           1 206 896 bytes
                             248 832 bytes free

[root@localhost modules]#
```

FIGURE 13-4 Listing of Linux boot files

Step 3   After rebooting with the disk in the drive, you should have seen the LILO screen. To boot into Linux, you should have simply typed **Linux** at the prompt. Figure 13-5 shows the LILO screen after the proper input.

Lab Solution 13.05

The following steps allow you to install the Apache web server:

Step 1   You should have inserted CD2 of the Red Hat Installation CDs.

Step 2   You should have mounted the CD with the **mount /mnt/cdrom** command. You should have changed to the RPMS directory with **cd /mnt/cdrom/RedHat/RPMS**.

Step 3   You should have entered **ls apa*** to see all files associated with the Apache server. You should have then installed these packages with **rpm -ivh apa***. While the files are installing, you should have seen the screen shown in Figure 13-6, which indicates the progress of the files.

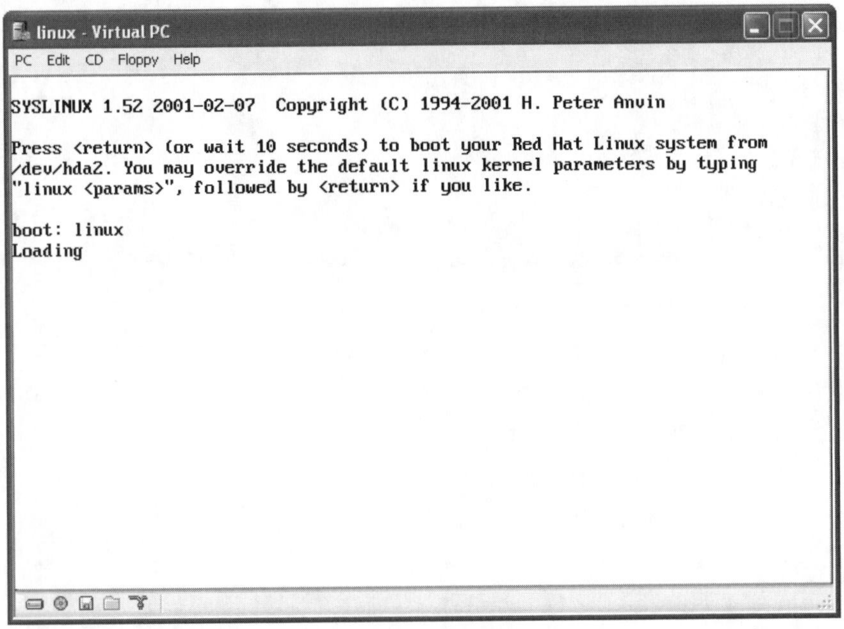

FIGURE 13-5 LILO boot screen

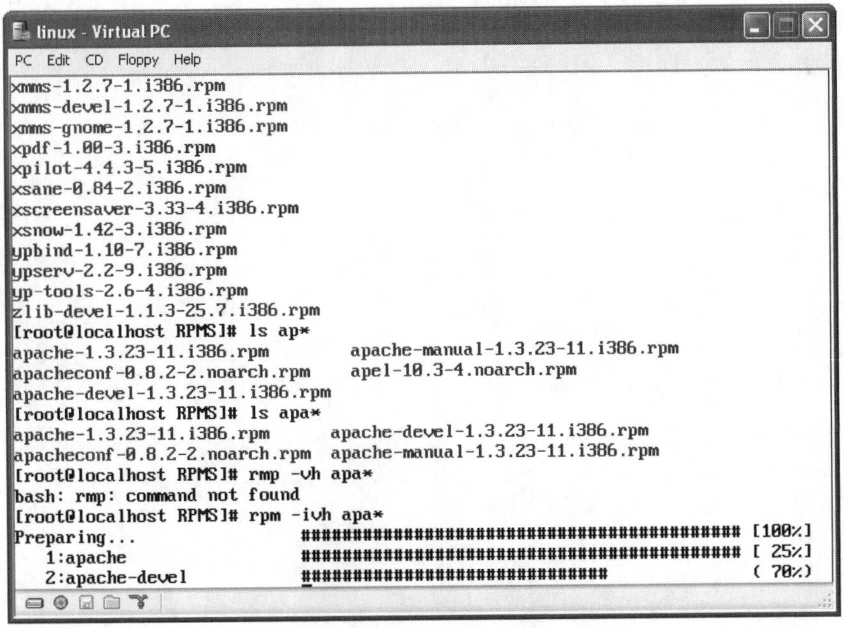

FIGURE 13-6 Installing Apache

Index

Symbols

A

INTERNATIONAL CONTACT INFORMATION

AUSTRALIA
McGraw-Hill Book Company Australia Pty. Ltd.
TEL +61-2-9900-1800
FAX +61-2-9878-8881
http://www.mcgraw-hill.com.au
books-it_sydney@mcgraw-hill.com

CANADA
McGraw-Hill Ryerson Ltd.
TEL +905-430-5000
FAX +905-430-5020
http://www.mcgraw-hill.ca

GREECE, MIDDLE EAST, & AFRICA
(Excluding South Africa)
McGraw-Hill Hellas
TEL +30-1-656-0990-3-4
FAX +30-1-654-5525

MEXICO (Also serving Latin America)
McGraw-Hill Interamericana Editores S.A. de C.V.
TEL +525-117-1583
FAX +525-117-1589
http://www.mcgraw-hill.com.mx
fernando_castellanos@mcgraw-hill.com

SINGAPORE (Serving Asia)
McGraw-Hill Book Company
TEL +65-863-1580
FAX +65-862-3354
http://www.mcgraw-hill.com.sg
mghasia@mcgraw-hill.com

SOUTH AFRICA
McGraw-Hill South Africa
TEL +27-11-622-7512
FAX +27-11-622-9045
robyn_swanepoel@mcgraw-hill.com

SPAIN
McGraw-Hill/Interamericana de España, S.A.U.
TEL +34-91-180-3000
FAX +34-91-372-8513
http://www.mcgraw-hill.es
professional@mcgraw-hill.es

UNITED KINGDOM, NORTHERN,
EASTERN, & CENTRAL EUROPE
McGraw-Hill Education Europe
TEL +44-1-628-502500
FAX +44-1-628-770224
http://www.mcgraw-hill.co.uk
computing_neurope@mcgraw-hill.com

ALL OTHER INQUIRIES Contact:
Osborne/McGraw-Hill
TEL +1-510-549-6600
FAX +1-510-883-7600
http://www.osborne.com
omg_international@mcgraw-hill.com